SCOURGE

Confronting the Global Issue of Addiction

by

Bradford Smith

Published

Olivia Kimbrell Press™

Copyright Notice

Scourge: Confronting the Global Issue of Addiction

This book is a work of nonfiction. Specific names and places of individuals and towns may have been changed in order to protect the privacy of those involved or where required by law in the case of minor children.

PUBLISHED BY: Olivia Kimbrell Press™*, P.O. Box 4393, Winchester, KY 40392-4393

The *Olivia Kimbrell Press™* colophon and open book logo are trademarks of Olivia Kimbrell Press™. **Olivia Kimbrell Press™ is a publisher offering true to life, meaningful fiction from a Christian worldview intended to uplift the heart and engage the mind.*

Original Cover Art and Graphics by Debi Warford (www.debiwarford.com)

Library Cataloging Data
U.S. Library of Congress Control Number: 2014949653
Smith, Bradford. (Bradford Smith) 1973-
Scourge; Confronting the Global Issue of Addiction/Bradford Smith
208 p. 20.32cm x 12.7cm (8in x 5in.)
Summary: First hand accounts of those affected by addiction as witnessed by a foster family. Includes bibliographical references.

ISBN: 978-1-939603-55-5 (trade perfect) ISBN: 978-1-939603-54-8 (ebook)
ISBN: 978-1-939603-57-9 (trade perfect POD)
1. Christian nonfiction 2. Recovery 3. Addiction 4. Fostering 5. Adoption 6. Drug abuse 7. Alcohol abuse 8. Biblical worldview

BV4527 SCGIA 2014 09
248.8'43—dc211

SCOURGE

Confronting the Global Issue of Addiction

by

Bradford Smith

TABLE OF CONTENTS

ACKNOWLEDGEMENTS

I want to thank … Christ the Lord ... His glory, His honor, His name.

And Ami…my best friend, confidant, and beautiful bride

INTRODUCTION

ALL men carry a burden. Imagine if you will, a man walking while carrying an immense weight on his shoulders, a heavy bag perhaps, or even a large rock or log. Some will carry it further and longer than others, depending upon their size, strength, and stamina. Yet, all will eventually falter. Imagine again that this same man cannot set the burden down, that no one will take it from him, a seemingly hopeless and desperate situation. In this case, the burden will eventually drive the strongest of men to their knees. The sheer *immutability* of the burden will necessarily crush even those possessing unmatched strength and stamina.

Now, imagine if you will that same man, carrying the same burden. Only this time, imagine that a cord or a whip or a snare of some kind lashes him about the legs. As his legs become bloodied and weakened by the lashing, the burden crushes him in the exact same way, but much, much sooner than if he had not endured the lashing about. It saps his strength, diminishes his stamina. It greatly lessens his ability to bear the burden. I seek to address, at least initially, this lashing about, reserving discussion on the burden for later. I must address the burden, just not at first.

You may find it startling to learn that even without a burden, even if someone or something has relieved the man of the burden — someonc has taken it from him or he has set it down — when lashed about in a similar fashion, he will still eventually find himself driven to his knees, this time by the sheer force of his own body weight coupled with the bloodying and weakening of his legs due to the lashing. His endurance becomes a function of his own strength as much as a function of the nature and severity of the lashing about.

Imagine one last time, this same man, burdened, lashed about the legs, stumbling perhaps. Now, imagine scores of them, these men. Everywhere you look, there are men languishing, some under the burden, many without the burden, all lashed about the legs in some manner. To your left, a man struggles to his knees under the burden, grimacing, writhing in pain from the sheer agony of bearing this immutable weight. His legs are a bloody mess from the lashing. Over there you see another man. There you see another. Everywhere, the burden crushes men and the lashing about causes them to stumble ever quicker, whether burdened or not.

Here stands the Minister, observing from either one or more of several possible conditions. Perhaps the Minister himself suffers from his own lashing about. Maybe hesitancy and uncertainty overcome the Minister. What should he do? Should he try to take the burden from one of the men? Should he throw himself in front of the lashing? Should he try and help the men bear the burden? The overwhelming volume of those suffering under the burden seemingly renders the Minister ineffective, at least as far as he is concerned.

A third and more odious condition may be that the Minister steadfastly ignores the struggle. Perhaps the busyness of life distracts him or he finds it much too distasteful to get involved in so sordid an affair lest he too become bloodied. After all, others more qualified than he could certainly better rend assistance. And still men falter, constantly.

Urgency becomes the driving consideration. As I dallied about editing this work, the sheer urgency of the situation overcame me. Urgency inundates and defines the very nature of the Struggle.

Shortly after receiving the Word of God in faith and declaring my submission to the Lord Jesus, an unmistakable, unshakable compelling need to proclaim the Gospel truths of which I had only recently become acquainted developed within me. Just as compelling, an overwhelming and ever-increasing desire recently developed within me; a desire to declare the truth of the matter of which I am about to proclaim, the commission of a warning and a call to action.

As I have come to know the peace of God which surpasses every thought, I have simultaneously become increasingly aware of the vast and bitter struggle that permeates the realm of all mankind. The Way is one of struggle, one of misery quite often, and it would seem that humanity, the *Cosmos*, exists perpetually immersed in a number of vicious struggles, all designed to ironically prevent humanity from joining the actual struggle that counts, the struggle that matters most. The struggle has levels, different aspects, but at some point, the levels become indistinguishable from one another, at least to the one struggling. Immediacy prompts our attention, demanding urgency. As such, the burden becomes reconciled with existence — it just is - while the lashing about, though important and dreadful, demands focus due to its immediacy and the acute severity of the pain and suffering it rends.

Frequently, as one becomes increasingly aware of the extent of the struggle, calluses may develop on the soul, perhaps even over top of one's own scar tissue. *What difference could I possibly make?* For me, I must confess that there are times where I cry out to God, "When, O when LORD are you going to come and set things right?" I must confess that I wrestle with engagement on occasion, as the struggle rages around me so vicious and bitter.

A man walked into our church a number of months ago, homeless, living in a car with his wife and two children, nowhere to go, afflicted by the Scourge. The sheer hopelessness of his situation overcame me. We did what we could at that time; we put them up in a hotel for a few nights so that they at least had a safe place to sleep, invited them into our fellowship. Predictably, they disappeared back from whence they came almost as quickly as they arrived. *Did it even matter? Where were they now?* These questions, in the face of the seeming hopelessness of the Scourge, plague me.

I've wondered if theology might answer these questions. I've witnessed the dual-headed beast of orthodoxy, of those deeply embedded in ivory towers of righteousness as well as those literally trudging the proverbial and actual swampy morass of pitiful human existence to alleviate many of the burden. How can an idea permeate the fabric of existence? He has given us the Answer but at the same time has enabled us unto destruction of the self, in Sovereignty, equipping the adversary with a puzzling array of weaponry, abetted by the sheer flippant nature of fickle human will. The whitewashed halls of orthodoxy are often oblivious to life on the street, to the sheer gritty reality of the burden. Not that orthodoxy should ever be neglected or trivialized but the simple reality remains that few in the gutter consider it relevant or even consider it at all.

Yet, the deep things of God are not irrelevant or inconsequential to life on the street. Christ has always dwelt and worked in the flesh *and* in the spirit. He healed the sick and the lame, physically. He forgave sin, spiritual healing as it were. As such, how can one neglect either at the expense of the other? This tale of struggle at every level of existence permeates every aspect of the reality that the Word so clearly defines, the realm of the physical and the realm of the spiritual. Those realms mesh in the image of those thus stricken, those struggling under the burden and the lashing about.

This notion, the coalescing of the spiritual and physical aspects of affliction, speaks as equally and consistently from the funeral of a lost person to the loathsome image of the drunken wretch lying in a pool of his own vomit, neither one having been aware, perhaps, of the existence of these distinct realities or at least of their collusion. The drunkard, dulled as he has become, suffers likely un-tuned to the things of the spirit whereas the lost dies *willingly* aware of little other than the physical, though he may possess a perverted or murky pseudo-understanding of a vague spirituality.

In all of this, God calls the man of faith, the Minister, to a unique existence, a duality, an awareness and engagement in each reality, physical and spiritual. He inextricably intertwines these aspects of man's existence. To divorce oneself from either aspect effectively negates engagement in the other. I hope to sound the clarion call, a call to a totality of engagement, to which if even one were to respond, I would consider it all joy in heaven.

CHAPTER ONE

The Courtroom

MY wife and I sat in court a number of months ago and could not help noticing a particular young woman a couple of rows in front of us. Her appearance was startling. I remember that she looked very skinny — too skinny — in that particular way that only a very ill person looks.

You know what I'm talking about here, where someone's elbows are actually bigger around than the meaty part of their arms. She was dirty and disheveled. Her clothes were wrinkled and stained. Her dirty-blonde hair was long and oily, matted. Her skin was very pale — sickly pale — with little scabs all over her neck and face.

Even as shocking as she looked, her appearance didn't first draw our notice. It wasn't how she looked that caused us to really notice her. It was how she *acted* that truly captured our attention.

She stood up. She sat down. She stood back up. She looked around. She sat back down. She touched her face. She put her hand back down. She touched her face again, looked around again, and stood back up again.

It was apparent that even if she had wanted to this woman *could not* sit still. Clearly agitated, she was powerless to sit quietly in court. Obviously, she was not moving of her own volition. Something drove her to move. Something compelled her to move.

Have you ever seen someone deep in the throes of addiction? Chemical addiction obviously bound this woman, imprisoning her in a prison with no walls, a prison from which few escape. We were witnessing the symptoms, the physical manifestations of the Scourge.

I remember thinking she looked like a car wreck. After a wreck, one can normally still recognize the car as a car. You'd be hard pressed to observe the aftermath of even the most horrific of car wrecks and not still realize, "I'm looking at a car." But after a wreck a car usually does not resemble what the original designer of the car had in mind. While still recognizable as a car, the sheer awful physics of the impact have distorted and twisted the entire frame.

That's how this woman looked. I mean, here was the very *Imago Dei*, the *Image of God*, still recognizable as a human being, but distorted and twisted by the sheer awful realities of chemical addiction, the Scourge. Much like the car from the car accident, the Designer clearly did not have this in mind at creation, at least in the blueprints that He has revealed.

This woman looked like she had just returned from a battle or maybe even as if she still fought the battle. Consider the soldier fresh out of basic training: clean-haircut, pressed uniform, sparkly brass, shiny buttons, standing tall and proud. Now, contrast him with the battle-weary veteran returning from the front lines, unshaven, dirty, eyes bloodshot from lack of sleep, ragged looking uniform, no medals or brass or shiny buttons, perhaps limping from his wounds.

This woman was clearly, decisively engaged in a battle for her very life, for her very soul, with an Enemy seeking nothing less than her complete and total destruction.

Setting the Stage:

THROUGH certain circumstances I intend to describe I have come to know more than a few addicts and those intensely affected by addiction. I have learned that you cannot speak with any addict - or ex-addict, if there is such a thing - without them describing addiction as a war, a battle. Their very language speaks to the severity of the condition. Of course, many folks will use decidedly warlike language to describe many different things.

I've heard countless coaches describe the game of football as a battle or a war. I've heard politicians declare war on opposing politicians. We wage war against ideas, ideologies, icons, beliefs, and inanimate objects. Thus we've had the War on Drugs, the War on Crime, and the War on Poverty. The United States fought the War on Terror for well over a decade.

Nearly every addict I know will use warlike descriptive terms in describing his or her personal *battle* with substance abuse. This desperate struggle rages, a war that weakens, destroys, tearing families, people, and even nations to shreds.

I do not know what spiritual background or standing you possess or even whether you believe in spiritual matters. Up front, I am a professing believer and follower of my Savior, Christ the Lord, *Yeshua*, called Jesus of Nazareth. I am writing this from a Christian perspective and this work will certainly contain some decidedly Christian overtones because of my worldview.

Yet, even if you are not a Christian or a supplicant of any religion, I believe that examination of the issue of addiction from a spiritual perspective has great utility, if nothing more than to convince you of the severity and urgency of the situation. Do you have an open mind? You *could* be wrong after all and one would have great difficulty in denying that chemical addiction eats away at the core of people, nations, and fabric of societies.

I do not intend to wow you with stories of faith-based healings from addiction in the hope that you turn to the Christian faith, though to be fair, I cannot help but include an aspect of that very thing. However, you'll see that one of the accounts given is entirely un-Christian. This particular fellow first started out in a Christian-based rehabilitation program and when that didn't work, it was explained to him that he didn't have enough faith and that was why Jesus did not cure him of his addiction.

Needless to say, he was slightly soured on the Christian experience after that. He has since been clean from his addiction for almost two years now through, as he explains it, his own will with the help of a *higher power.*

One of my favorite theological quotes comes from the movie *The Usual Suspects*, a great work of biblical narrative and societal commentary. Obviously I'm joking here, but in it, the arch-criminal, Keyser Söze, makes the statement that the greatest trick the Devil ever pulled was convincing the world that he didn't exist.

I'm convinced that the Devil has succeeded in convincing humanity in the west of exactly this, that he doesn't exist. Americans, at least, suffer the oppression of satanic attack while not even acknowledging the existence of anything spiritual. If we do acknowledge the spiritual it's of a new-age variety of spirituality, many worshipping the *great whatever* or things that are abstractly spiritual.

Our postmodern world has cast aside the clearly defined and concrete spiritual truths of the Bible in favor of easy-believism, moral relativism, and an ever-growing population apathetic to things of a spiritual nature. Yet, the battle rages, whether you acknowledge it or not. The oblivion of the masses does not negate the reality of the battle.

If you read the Bible, if you follow the Bible, then you understand that humanity has a real enemy and that a spiritual battle rages around us all the time, every day. Indeed, as a Christian I perceive that *all* things have a spiritual nature to them.

One of the my favorite Bible verses from the Apostle Paul's letter to the church at Ephesus reminds me of this truth.

> For our battle is not against flesh and blood, but against the rulers, against the authorities, against the world powers of this darkness, against the spiritual forces of evil in the heavens.
>
> Ephesians 6:12

This work will focus upon this spiritual battle with respect to chemical addiction. Paul says it clearly and he writes from the perspective of one who was persecuted greatly for his faith. As he explains it in 2 Corinthians 11, he was imprisoned, beaten near death, beaten with a rod three times, whipped, stoned, shipwrecked, cold, tired and hungry.

Yet, Paul did not see the people doing these things *to him* as the enemy. His enemy was not flesh and blood. His enemy was not a person, even the people or persons who persecuted him. He fought a spiritual battle, an otherworldly battle.

How else would you expect an enemy of God, which the Bible calls all non-believers, to behave toward someone proclaiming the Gospel of Jesus Christ? Christians should expect this type of persecution from non-believers. Indeed, even as Paul explains it, if we are not persecuted at some point, then perhaps we are doing something wrong, keeping our faith a secret or living a carnal, worldly existence.

Why would the Enemy need to persecute you if you were no threat to him, if you were not furthering the Kingdom of God in some way?

Scripture speaks clearly to the matter; each and every one of us lives immersed in a spiritual battle every single day. It rages around us and Scripture speaks equally as clearly in that we have an enemy and his name is Satan. Make no mistake. Satan seeks our destruction. As Peter reminds us:

> Be Sober! Be on alert! Your adversary the Devil is prowling around like a roaring lion, looking for anyone he can devour.
>
> 1 Peter 5:8

Satan seeks our destruction. Make no mistake, Satan hates God. Satan seeks to supplant God. Satan rebelled against God, but he cannot harm God. In fact, Satan can do nothing without permission or allowance from God. Think of Job from the Old Testament.

> Have you considered my servant Job?

Since Satan cannot harm God, what better way to harm Him than to harm those made in His image, those that He loves. Yet most Christians live oblivious to this notion. The very idea of the person of Satan seems somehow antiquated, quaint, or even embarrassing. However, this does not negate the reality of his existence or the bitter struggle he wages against the people of God.

The War Against Christianity

DO you know when Islamic terrorists first attacked the mainland United States? In 1972, ten members of a local mosque in New York City made a phony emergency phone call and then gunned down the responding officers, killing one.[1] Since then, there have been dozens of attacks from Islamic terrorists against the mainland United States killing *thousands* of Americans, not to mention the dozens of attacks against Americans and American interests overseas. For nearly thirty years, Islamic terrorists waged a bitter war against the United States of America and the west, seeking its destruction.

In 1998 Osama bin Laden, the deceased leader of Al-Qaida, even issued a *fatwah*, a religious decree, whereby he publicly declared war on the United States.[2] The concept was simple, death by a thousand cuts. He realized that they could not defeat the United States militarily, force on force, so he directed his fighters to focus on consistent attacks against soft targets, primarily civilians. In his eyes, the idea of noncombatants didn't exist.

Yet, it wasn't until after the attacks of September 11th that the United States fought back. You see, Al-Qaida fought the United States long before the United States really returned fire. There were certainly limited responses, think Ronald Reagan and Muammar Gaddafi. Yet Al-Qaida fought a total war, a generational war, and still does today. For them, this was no skirmish.

The spiritual battle contains many of these same reflections. Satan and his minions wage a bitter war against humanity, but most do not fight back, at least in the west. Most live content to exist in the shallow pool of self-exalting humanism, gratifying the physical and denying the spiritual, while beneath the surface, behind the veil, the Enemy scores victory after victory. Every day, it seems that Satan gains ground in America and as we'll see, chemical addiction serves as a powerful tool in Satan's vast arsenal of weaponry.

Christians in the west, in America, possess a nasty tendency to look down our collective noses at ourselves at weak, western Christianity. We look around the world and we see our brothers and sisters in Christ literally fighting for their lives, persecuted to death.

Across large swaths of the globe, no one may utter the name of Jesus — no one may preach the Gospel message — and live. This is a fact. Persecutors send those that break ranks to prison. They murder people. They make people disappear. *They kill families.*

In Sudan, an Islamic court sentences a pregnant Christian

woman to death for the crime of professing Christ. In mercy, they allow her to live until she gives birth. In Iran, a Christian pastor languishes in prison for the crime of preaching Christ. In Somalia, gunmen pull a Christian woman from her home and gun her down in front of her family for the crime of being a Christian and renouncing Islam.

The forces of evil are waging a frontal assault against Christianity in many parts of the world: China, North Korea, most of the Middle East, Afghanistan, and Southeast Asia. Ironically though, the Church *thrives*. In places of the most intense persecution, and historically during times of intense persecution, the Church explodes. The Church, in many places the underground church just as in the days of Roman persecution, thrives where pressed the most. And supposedly soft Christians in the west look at this and see the plight of their brothers and sisters in Christ and ask, "C*ould I do that? Could I profess Christ under that kind of duress? Would I have enough faith?*"

We pray for those persecuted around the globe all the while feeling perhaps more than a tinge of guilt knowing that we possess the freedom they desire but perhaps do not make the full use of it as we know we ought. I possess perfect freedom to profess Christ consistently, openly, but I do not. No particular reason.

Yet, in another way, the battle in the west is much tougher.

The War on Western Culture

IN the west, the Enemy oppresses in a much subtler fashion, waging war discretely. Here in the west, you will not get your head cut off for professing Christ … yet. The Enemy persecutes in a different manner. Instead of a frontal assault, Satan busily orchestrates an envelopment, rolling up the flanks of a well-deceived enemy, the Church. Frequently the Church seems barely aware of this assault, focused instead upon any innumerable of peripheral issues while missing the actual enemy at the gates.

Certainly the nation in its entirety has no collective awareness of this onslaught, only a vague understanding that something is deeply wrong. We are not sure what, but most do recognize, even the secular, that something is very wrong, that things are not how they should be. Satan has employed and continues to employ an array of tricks and deceptions to oppress and afflict humanity in ways that most do not even recognize. In the west, in America, Satan uses the scourge of chemical addiction as but one of many subtle tactics that he possesses. Yet, the Scourge afflicts in a disturbingly effective manner, a manner worth addressing independently.

Consider the party scene, the club scene. The music blares, bass thumping. Bodies grind on the dance floor. Drinks flow. Neon lights. Flash and bling. Imminent hookups abound. This is just what people do, particularly young people, and besides, it's fun, harmless.

Behind the scenes though, if you pull back the curtain, lift the veil, you see the young man lying in a pool of his own vomit. You see the young woman raped by a friend while both were under the influence of alcohol. You see the families ripped apart, victims killed by those who decide to get behind the wheel while chemically impaired. You see the life-changing decisions people make while under the influence of chemicals. You see the progression from party to binge to habit and into the vortex of addiction as the Scourge runs its course toward destruction.

I seek to address this Scourge. It is subtle, devastating, a weapon so powerful that it threatens to rip apart the very fabric of this society. Am I exaggerating? Allow me to ask, how many people do you know who have had their lives changed irreparably as a result of chemical addiction or as a result of choices made while under the influence of chemicals? Are you one of them?

For reasons known only to Him, God has surrounded me with people battling this addiction and the longer I go on, the more I am convinced that Satan uses chemical addiction as a great and powerful weapon. I am utterly convinced that he uses addiction, chemical addiction, to oppress and afflict vast swaths of humanity. Alcohol, illegal drugs, prescription drugs, antidepressants, painkillers: they all possess the ability to afflict and enslave. Interestingly enough, those who battle these addictions, whether religious or not, not only describe it as a battle, but will willingly admit that they believe the Devil himself uses it to afflict.

In the Garden, the Enemy issued his own *fatwah*, his own declaration of war. May we do the same. Oh that we might become aware of and engaged in this fight, this battle, this struggle. Perhaps awareness will prompt engagement. I seek awareness with this work. Let us never hide behind collective professed ignorance. In that spirit, let's peer behind the curtain, into the battle as it rages. Look behind the veil.

CHAPTER 1 DISCUSSION

THIS book focuses on addicts, addiction, and the spiritual damage addiction brings.

1) Do you know someone who struggles with addiction? What do you know about that person?

2) Why are you reading this book? What do you intend to gain?

Read Ephesians 6:12 then pray over the following question.

3) What are some evil forces we routinely battle in our daily lives?

Genesis 3:15 is commonly referred to as the *Protoevangelium.*

4) What is the heel that Satan will bruise? Is that us? Mankind? Christians?

5) Based upon what you know about God, why would He include this in the curse?

6) Where has God called you to engage in the war? Have you been unaware of a spiritual attack before? Where has spiritual warfare resonated in your life to date?

CHAPTER TWO

CHAPTER TWO

The Midnight Caller

YOU could hardly imagine a more pathetic sight, and I do mean pathetic. Heartbreaking, actually. Midnight and there appears a blonde, five-year old little boy, clinging to a dirty stuffed animal, standing on the stoop in front of the door of a strange house full of strange people. He even had a little Walmart bag with some clothes in it to complete the picture. He was scared to death — terrified — with silent tears running down his dirty cheeks. He clung to the caseworker's leg.

This scene greeted my beloved bride, Ami, when she answered the door in the dead of night. This was her first glimpse of our second foster child who just hours before had seen his family ripped apart at its very seams by the evil whims of addiction. Here was affliction firsthand, live, 3-D, in the flesh. Ironically enough, I was safely tucked away in Iraq at the time, but my wife remembers it like it was yesterday.

That moment in time is frozen in our lives like a waypoint, a touchstone, an old fashioned photograph. That moment, that little boy, would lead our family to his biological mother, Ms. Laurel.

Recently, as I was preparing to preach a sermon from John chapter 5 whereby Jesus heals the lame man by the pool in Bethesda, I reflected on the afflictions that plague this nation.Quite naturally, I began to think of drug and alcohol abuse. The focus of my sermon was on Jesus' mission to heal and to save and I felt led to ask Ms. Laurel to give her testimony (to our family she is and always will be Ms. Laurel).

Ms. Laurel agreed to speak and it was amazing. What was even more amazing was the several hours I got to spend with her sitting in my garage/office as she poured out her story. One of the most candid and sincere people I have ever met, Ms. Laurel speaks completely earnestly, always forthcoming in her struggles and tribulations and triumphs. Yet, I wasn't even in the country when Ms. Laurel first introduced herself into our lives. It was her son that my family met first, as my wonderful wife, Ami, relayed to me.

Miss Laurel

ADMITTEDLY, much of Ms. Laurel's life dwells in a haze, memories lost forever to a drunken, drug-induced fog that casts a pall over many of her years. Really, her earliest memory is from the fourth grade when her mother left her fourth husband for number five and then six, the same man those last two times, and in the process moved her and Laurel straight to Sin City, Las Vegas.

The contrast was stark. Before, it had been Catholic school, with no-kidding nuns and priests. Now it was lots of unsupervised time while Laurel's mom worked or gambled. With little or no supervision, young Laurel naturally began hanging with the older kids, stealing money from her mom's purse to buy cigarettes from the nearby cigarette machine. It was then that she first started smoking pot with an older kid … and drinking. As she stated, though, "there were lots of blank spots, lots of moving around."

Laurel could tell that something was missing. She wanted to know her Dad for one thing. "Maybe this person will care about me." So that summer, she went and visited him in Pennsylvania and had a great time.

Now, her Dad was a heavy drinker and drug user, an addict. So Laurel would watch him have parties and he would take her with him to the bar where she would sit and drink tomato juice. Partying became associated with fun. She would even drive him home from the bar, well before she had a license.

Unfortunately, the fun did not last. In her 7th grade year, her Dad beat her up pretty good. He and his girlfriend had an actual physical altercation. So he left for three days leaving Laurel at home with no food, no vehicle, and as she remembered, no air conditioning. She would sit, staring out the window, waiting for him to come home. She actually saw him go by the house a couple of times before he finally came home.

The girlfriend had just finished making breakfast when he walked in and immediately started in on her. Laurel, not wanting to see him hit her anymore, threw her toast at him. Her Dad looked at her, handed his cigarette to the girlfriend saying, "Hold it or eat it," and he came after Laurel.

She found herself kicking and fighting and he hit her. She ran into the bedroom and he followed. As she cowered in the corner, he kicked her, hard, so hard that he separated the meat on her ribs from the bone. Fittingly enough, school pictures were the very next day and Laurel got the honor of taking hers with a distinct black eye from her father. Her mother came and got her right after that.

Immersion

SHORTLY thereafter, her uncle, a businessman in Philadelphia, offered to let her live there. He had a daughter who was one year older than Laurel and a son who was one year younger. From the beginning, she blended in well there.

The older daughter was beautiful and popular and lots of older boys hung. The drinking and partying went on nearly nonstop, especially when the uncle was out of town on business.

It was there, in the 9th grade, Laurel was introduced to cocaine.

The parties were memorable, what she could remember of them. Everyone was drinking, smoking pot, and snorting cocaine, including Laurel. The guys would bring it over. People had acid. At one party in particular, everyone was on acid, though as Laurel explained, that was not her thing. But cocaine was her thing. She fell in love with it from the very first line. It changed the way she felt; it was better than any feeling she'd ever had so she did it as frequently as possible.

Life continued like this for the next several years until Laurel's cousin graduated from high school and so, in the spirit of the wild and free young Americans, they packed up the car and drove from Pennsylvania to California, partying the whole way there. They rented an apartment in a beautiful complex and it was here that Laurel was first introduced to crystal methamphetamine. She stayed on meth for two years straight. Her cousin eventually left California but Laurel stayed there with her mother.

Her senior year, she fell asleep while driving and was in a terrible accident. The steering wheel shattered her nose, teeth, and cheeks requiring over 70 stitches in her mouth but she was a trooper. None of that stopped her from doing crystal meth.

At this time, Laurel's Uncle Steve, her dad's brother in San Diego, offered to let her come and recuperate and so she did. Well, at least she went and stayed. As Laurel explained it, Uncle Steve was her favorite. He was cool and she adored him. He also did crystal meth and grew his own marijuana. Everything was free. They went to Tijuana almost every weekend. The party continued. Laurel was having fun and was still able to maintain a job.

Eventually she went back to her mother's house. She had quit school shortly after the accident at the age of 16. How could she go back to school looking like that; her boyfriend even dumped her because of the accident. Pregnant with his child, she opted for an abortion. But, she was young and cute, weighing a mere 82 pounds, always attracting a lot of attention from the boys.

Her mom however had different ideas. She told her that whatever she was on, she needed to get off, because she looked like she was going to die. So she did. Meth had really begun to mess her up. She was sick all the time, unable to eat. It was really starting to get ahold of her, so she quit … doing meth, but returned to her original drug of choice, alcohol.

Thus the cycle that would haunt her for the vast majority of her life continued. She was never abstinent from at least one substance. For over two decades she took some form of chemical every single day, without exception.

Tiring of California, Laurel ended up back in Philadelphia with her uncle, doing a lot of cocaine, but holding a steady job. She really felt like she had *it* under control as she trained to be a dental assistant. She had a really nice boyfriend at the time and though they would go out often, she did not party nearly as much as she used to. She was much more interested in him than her dope.

It was then that she got a phone call from her Dad in Meadville, Pa who had just had a baby with his girlfriend and so she closed her checking account, quit her job, packed up the car and went to her Dad's and to see her new baby sister. She decided to stay.

In Meadville, she got into bartending and was very good at it which is not surprising. A cute, young girl who knows how to party and make good drinks would certainly be a draw. She bartended for years and at one point was even recruited between bars. At this point, Laurel got involved with a cocaine dealer. She knew he partied, but had no idea how big he actually was. And so she would go to work every day and it was all the cocaine that you wanted, free. All of the bartenders were high and things began to spiral out of control. That was when she first met Craig, her girls' dad.

Baby on the Way

CRAIG would sit at the end of the bar and talk to her the whole shift and he kept asking her out. Laurel was not interested, but finally one day, he brought her a gold chain and since it was apparent he wasn't giving up, she agreed to go out with him. Craig and Laurel dated for three months and though she was on the pill, she became pregnant with her oldest daughter. Though she stopped using cocaine during her pregnancy she smoked pot the whole time and drank some as well.

But she was very excited about the baby. Laurel expected Craig to straighten right up after her daughter was born, but he never really did making a few halfhearted attempts.

She fell into depression and began self-medicating, beginning a new destructive pattern as she would leave her baby with her parents and go out, bartending, partying, returning to her former lifestyle with a vengeance. About this time, the coke dealer got busted and most of the cocaine left town so everyone started smoking crack, which was readily available.

Laurel hated it. She didn't like the smell or the taste of it and as she put it, she was the last one to give it a try. She finally took a hit and that was all it took. From then on, chasing the next high was all she cared about. It was an incredibly powerful feeling. From the age of 26 to 39, for 13 years, crack cocaine held her prisoner, "dragged her by the butt" as she would say.

Crack was different. Laurel didn't know what it was, maybe how it was ingested. Most users smoke crack normally, but you can inject it, which gives a different feeling. How you put it in your body produces a decidedly different effect. She found it seductive and powerful and as she explained, "once it has ahold of you, it will not let go," as evidenced by her impending 13 year battle.

I've been to five 28 day programs, detox twice, OD'd twice in the hospital.

I've had a heart infection … those times, those years, were so in-and-out, very sick times, incomprehensible demoralization … I've done things I never would have dreamed of … stolen things, slept with people, manipulated people, given away cars, driven drug dealers into the heart of the cities to scary places, pawned things, lied to get money, lied to mom, lied to Craig's dad, who was a big enabler.

He knew what I was doing. He gave me money so I wouldn't have to prostitute, which I would've done, and turned the other cheek. I've left my children alone, taken them with me, been high in the same home. They're not dumb, they can see the change, they knew something was not right with mom. I've pawned my kids off on my family. I would leave to get milk or cigs and come back three days later … the first hit would be all it would take and I wouldn't stop until I was physically exhausted and had exhausted all resources.

I lost job after job, lost relationships, respect for myself, respect for others. I've been to jail, arrested in 1998 for misdemeanor possession of cocaine, busted for one line, one line, which was amazing after all of the coke I'd done. I went to a crack house in the middle of a sting operation, got busted. They wanted me to rat on people, but I wouldn't do it … got probation. I was arrested in 2005 for taking the wrong purse out of a bar; I was so drunk during an outing with some girlfriends.

I've been to jail a total of four times, numerous probation violations. I just couldn't stay clean and pass urine tests … terrible, unhealthy relationships. I chose to be with men in that life, living that lifestyle who also did drugs, sick unhealthy, relationships … I was verbally, emotionally, and physically abused and I put out that on others as well. My friends and the courts suggested some of my early treatments.

I wanted to stop and be a good mom and stop being a

> drug addict mom. I would go to treatment. It felt good in there. I'd start eating. That's where I learned that I had a disease when all along I had thought that I was just evil. I did not want to leave treatment because I knew what would happen when I did.
>
> Once out, I would start going to meetings, starting looking and feeling better, get a job, begin repairing relationships, mom would stop being sad, Craig would start talking to me and then, out of the blue, ... I would want to get high more than I wanted to stay sober and the whole thing would start all over again.

Laurel met Lyle in jail. He was the son of a friend of hers. Their romance was quick as they were married and soon had a son. Lyle struggled with his own demons and so they decided to move to Arizona to live with his parents. There were more jobs and just too many bad influences in Meadville. Everyone in Lyle's family drank and used, so they headed west with their son. Shortly after arriving, Lyle enlisted in the Army without telling her about it and was shipped off to basic training and AIT where he was gone for nearly a year. After AIT, he got stationed at Fort Campbell, Kentucky.

For Laurel though, the demons of addiction continued to haunt her. It was about this time that it became apparent to her that, "*No human power could save me*."

No Human Power

IT had taken her a long time, decades to figure this out. She had always wanted her mom or her dad to fix her. Maybe if she had the right guy or the right house or the right job, things would be okay, but even when she had that stuff, things were never okay. All the experiences and processes led her to the point where she learned it was not about losing husbands and jobs and houses and friends, but that this affliction truly wanted to kill her and it would if she didn't do something about it. Something was missing, but Laurel did not know what it was.

She prayed. She prayed hard. In her affliction she turned to God as so many others do. She asked God to show her what she needed to do and she became convinced that somehow, she needed to turn her life over to Him. She had to find a way to do that, but didn't know how. Enter God, via Ami Smith and Shannon the case worker.

The night that Logan was taken was a huge turning point for Laurel and, in retrospect, she is glad that it affected her the way it did. She had seen it before. Other addict mothers were sad when their kids were taken but the sad reality was that it just gave them that much more freedom to destroy themselves, to continue in pursuit of the high.

It's not that they don't love their kids, but that is the power of the Scourge. Laurel desperately did not want to be in that category but to her shame, she got high the very night Logan was taken. However, she woke up the next morning determined, so she cleared her phone contacts, threw out her paraphernalia, and forsook all of the people who were her enablers, but she still found herself wanting to get high. They had her kid, but she wanted the high. It tore at her.

Suicide entered Laurel's mind. Logan would be better off without her. She couldn't see how life could get any better. There was no light at the end of the tunnel. Everything was dark and too hard. It just wasn't possible. It was going to kill her anyway and if she was going to die, then she might as well get it over with instead of suffering this long, slow, agonizing death.

But she didn't. She called her DCS case worker, Shannon, and told her she was scared. So, she got checked into a stabilization unit for a few days where she was diagnosed with bipolar disorder, general anxiety disorder, borderline personality disorder, and clinical depression. Once Laurel got checked in and got on some medication, she started feeling better. While there, she was praying mightily for God to please make a way. She knew that if she was going to live, it was going to be because God made a way for her. *No human power could save her.*

Laurel was in the facility for three days. She had nowhere to go. She had lost everything, her house, her son, her husband. She only had the clothes on her back, so Shannon took her into her home.

That's who God sent, Shannon the case worker.

The Case Worker and the Foster Mother

IT was awesome. For three months, Shannon put her up, against DCS policy. She could have gotten fired over it. Laurel was shocked over where help had finally come from and did not know what she would have done without her.

That's when she started talking to Ami. Ami called her the day after they took Logan. Needless to say, Laurel was a mess. She had no idea where Logan was or who he was with or if she would ever get him back or if she could stay sober. She was alone, upset about Lyle who had called DCS in the first place during a drunken fight, and had lost everything. Again, it was a very dark hour.

But then Ms. Ami called (though Laurel is older than Ami she still to this day refers to her as Ms. Ami). Ami told her that she had Logan and that he was okay and that she could only imagine how she felt and that she and her husband, me, would do whatever we could to help her get her son and her life back, to get stable again.

> I can't even explain how I knew, but it was the hugest God moment ever.
>
> I can't explain the feeling, like He sent someone. Ami made it easy for me to be comfortable; she shared with me about how she used to be and how she was this close to being in the same shoes. She honestly

> cared for me when I didn't think anyone else in the world did.
>
> I lost my whole family. They were tired of hearing me say, 'I'm sorry, I'll try' and my words just didn't mean anything to them anymore.

So Laurel started hanging around my family a lot. She started going to church with us and still remembers the first sermon she heard from Brother Larry, the pastor at Hilldale Baptist Church. She had brought her boyfriend, Bo, and Larry preached on adultery. Laurel swore that Larry was preaching directly to her. "It was terrible", she confesses with a smile.

Laurel started going to AA meetings, got a sponsor, and began to get serious about working the program. She had a really good sponsor who painted a very clear picture for her. It was either life or death. You are going to die. You are killing yourself. You have two options, continue to the bitter end and die a miserable death or live and claim blessings beyond belief.

Laurel had made a decision to try, for real. She got to the third step in the twelve pretty quickly, the third step being to turn your life over to the will and power of God as she understood it and so on that day, at Hilldale Baptist Church in Clarksville, Tennessee, Laurel went forward at the invitation and surrendered her life to Jesus Christ and she meant it with her whole heart.

As she professes, her life has been completely different since, but not all easy. Her last relapse was perhaps her worst and perhaps the scariest. While working through her recovery, Laurel became obsessed by her job. It became her life. She stopped going to meetings or seeing her sponsor. The job became more important and she missed all hints from Logan, whom she had gotten back, and her husband.

One weekend, her two daughters came to visit from Pennsylvania and when she went to take them home, she was one week from being sober for a year, never having made it past six months before, when Lyle disappeared. As it turns out, he was with another waitress from work but Laurel wanted him to be with her. Yet, he wanted to drink. She didn't want to lose Lyle and so she cried, but said okay, come home and we'll drink and they did. It just took a second with no regrets, no seeking God's will, they would just drink.

Unfortunately things escalated pretty quickly from there. Addiction always progresses; you never go backwards and Laurel was able to pick up right where she had left off. I remember this weekend very vividly. We had Logan at our house but had no idea of Lyle or Laurel's whereabouts. One day became two and then three. We didn't know what to do knowing that if we called the police, they would take Logan from her again, so we prayed, hard.

The chain of events of that weekend, which are still foggy, led to Lyle leaving again as he fell back into his own addictions, smoking crack. He packed up his bags and left, never to return. The weekend scared Laurel so badly that she quit her job, went back to the meetings, and swore to do everything different.

Ever since, she has worked the AA program aggressively, listened to her sponsor, accepted the hard truths, worked the steps, and learned to apply them in life. This was huge for her, learning to apply what she had learned to her life situations. She had to make a decision every single day to give her life to God. "I'm not in control of anything. My best thinking got me where I was."

> I see God work in my life and everybody's life. I don't do things perfectly but I am a lot better mother, better character. When I say I will do something, I do it. When it comes to the 12 steps, I don't miss appointments or anything like that. I try to be of service to others. We don't get to keep what we get.
>
> My life is amazing. Material things are nice though I've never had a lot before. Now I have a car, a ring, nice

> things. I've never had someone who cares about me like this (speaking of her fiancé, Del), but it feels good. I have peace in my heart and soul, knowing that I would be okay with or without a man. This was the best gift from God ever.
>
> I always thought it was somebody else's responsibility to make me happy. It is okay when I am alone today. Before, I always had to have someone, codependent.

So Laurel started school. She prayed to God for the strength to go to school and to do something different and better and to stand on her own two feet financially and to take care of her children because that had always been a problem. She knew she couldn't do it without God and so He did; He gave her the will to take this test and go to school. God helped her overcome the fear. Laurel was terrified like never before. She was terrified of responsibility, terrified of success. She didn't know how to live right or behave right.

"God has given me unbelievable strength. If you would've asked me two years ago to get in front of the church to speak … no way. I don't speak well anyway, but it's not about me. You asked me to give a message and so I want to be a channel for my God. Though I am scared, I'll still do it," Laurel confessed to me as we were preparing her testimony for church.

Things have changed throughout Laurel's family. She is in a wonderful relationship with her fiancé. Her father stopped everything. He hasn't had a drink in years. Her uncle doesn't use nor does her mother. Eventually Laurel made amends with her parents, with her daughters, finding it a miracle that they still even speak to her.

Her youngest daughter, Olivia, she considers a true miracle. At that time, she did not want to be pregnant and so she behaved as if she wasn't. She smoked crack, drank, smoked weed the whole time until the last month of her pregnancy until the reality of what she was doing set it. Amazingly, Olivia was born perfectly healthy and normal in every way. Yet, guilt frequently overcomes her, especially whenever Olivia is sick or in trouble. All of her children have suffered greatly from her neglect and she feels incredibly grateful that they all still love her.

> I never knew how to have friends before without wanting something from them. People were a resource.
>
> When you are an alcoholic, you are in survival mode. Addicts are takers. We walk all over people to get what we want. I never wanted to hurt anyone, I just didn't feel. I blamed everyone else, Mom, Dad, Craig, Lyle. Only recently have I learned to take responsibility for what I have done and for what I do.
>
> I do all of that today. I can say I was sorry. I used to justify what I did. What I did was your fault, but I've done a lot of self-examination.

What she discovered was striking in its simplicity. *No human power could save me ...*

CHAPTER 1 DISCUSSION

THE book of Isaiah 46:9-10 says:

Remember what happened long ago,
for I am God, and there is no other;
I am God, and no one is like Me.
I declare the end from the beginning,
and from long ago what is not yet done,
saying: My plan will take place,
and I will do all My will.

1) What do these verses say about the sovereignty of God?

2) How do you account for the evil that happens in the world? The seemingly 'bad' things? Does God ordain evil?

3) How do you see sovereignty manifest itself in Laurel's life?

Ms. Laurel actually asked my wife at some point, "How do you become a Christian?"

> 4) Have you ever been asked this question? If so, how did you answer? How would you answer?
>
> 5) How do you present the Gospel? What themes must be consistent to be considered as the Gospel? What biblical texts could be used to assist?

Ms. Laurel was an addict for over twenty years; not a day passed that she didn't consume some sort of substance.

> 6) What would you say to someone who has been afflicted for the entirety of their lives who is perhaps even unaware of their affliction?
>
> 7) Do you know someone similarly afflicted? Have you done anything about it? If so, what? How did it go?

CHAPTER THREE

CHAPTER THREE

Hello, My Name Is ...

IF you have never been to an Alcoholics Anonymous meeting, I highly encourage you to find one and attend. They are very easy to find. Don't worry, they have no prerequisites or requirements. You may attend totally anonymous, hence the name, without being singled out in any way. In fact, this seems to be one of the strengths of the program. It is truly low-threat. One may attend on the periphery as long as desired and when ready and comfortable, embrace the program and get involved.

I was fortunate enough, along with my wife and girls, to attend an Alcoholic Anonymous meeting for Ms. Laurel's one year sober celebration. I must say that this experience humbled me spiritually, more perhaps than anything I had ever experienced before. Here, the scourge confronted me in person. I got a taste of affliction by spending an evening with those who valiantly battled these demons of the Scourge.

They welcomed us graciously, as if we were VIP's or distinguished guests. They showered us with love and attention making Ami and I, along with my girls, feel absolutely at ease and at home. Now, I must admit that I possessed some preconceived notions. How could I not? Don't you? Yet, the meeting turned out to be nothing like I expected. Second — and this humbled me the most — I discovered that these people were just like you and me. "Well, how can that be?" you may possibly ask. "You don't even know me."

The reason I can say with utmost confidence that these people were just like you and me is that the meeting drew people from every, and I do mean every, walk of life, all in various stages of the battle with the Scourge. This realization blew me away. I conversed with the stereotypical addicted *looking* people of course, much like our young woman from the courthouse, but I also spoke to very well-dressed people, obviously with money as well as many normal *looking* people.

I saw women. I saw men. I sat with young people. I spoke to old people. Married people were shepherding their children here and there. Single people were talking amongst themselves. Soldiers in uniform chatted idly with schoolteachers and lawyers. Homeless people mingled with the affluent. White people, brown people, black people, yellow people and various other shades, united by the commonality of battling the demons of addiction, all came together to support one another in this bitter struggle.

A quick look around the parking lot revealed all that you needed to know. BMW's sat alongside minivans and pickup trucks with motorcycles nestled in between.

They all battled addictions as varied as they themselves were. We obviously heard from alcoholics and drug addicts. We also heard from those addicted to prescription pain medications. Almost all of them confessed addictions to more than one substance. Many had not yet begun to fight, had not yet engaged in the battle. Some had just begun the fight, had just entered their initial battle, or perhaps had just realized that the battle actually existed, having been previously unaware.

Several spoke about struggling for decades, for their entire life. Some had not drank alcohol or done any drugs for years, but as they explained so fearlessly, once an addict, always an addict. It seems that though you may become clean, you are always an addict. Always. It never leaves you.

It humbled me, looking around this room, seeing the diversity of people all battling the same demons, the same evil, the demons of chemical addiction. It became apparent to me, in that instant, that addiction - for the purposes of this work, I'll speak to addiction as a generalization for all chemical addictions - but addiction knows no social barriers. Addiction does not discriminate. Addiction crosses barriers and boundaries as easily as you or I cross the street. Addiction is a great equalizer. All are equally powerless before the demons of addiction.

The businessman has no more power than the homeless person. The soldier has no more power than the housewife. Addiction brings all of those afflicted to an equality of misery, a unity of sorrow. Though they may originate from different positions in life, the end-state for those afflicted is almost always the same — destruction.

Addiction is truly a great equalizer.

May It Please the Court ...

I'VE observed exactly this in the courthouse. My wife and I spend a lot of time in court for a variety of different reasons. As foster parents, we frequently attend court on behalf of our foster children and their biological parents as they negotiate the foster system. We've also adopted a number of children and spent time in court for that reason.

Additionally, foster children also tend to require a fair amount of attention from the juvenile justice system for various manner of offenses — God bless them — and so that has required our presence in court on a number of occasions, supporting our foster children as they face various issues.

In court, I've made the exact same observations that I made at the Alcoholics Anonymous meeting. Those present for drug and alcohol related offenses are all cut from different types of cloth. There are no types!

I remember watching one particular exchange right in the hallway of the courthouse. An obviously addicted man, think again of the young woman from chapter one, engaged in some friendly conversation with another young man who wore a suit and looked like a banker. They exchanged some lighthearted banter but it soon became clear that the conversation had turned toward their various drug charges.

Here conversed two men, from seemingly different worlds, united by one thing, imminent and ongoing mutual destruction at the hand of chemical addiction. The man in the suit and the man in rags both possessed the same destiny, the same fate, courtesy of drug abuse, courtesy of the demons of chemical addiction.

Addiction is truly a great equalizer.

All Things Being Equal

SATAN has indeed found a weapon equally as effective against the rich as it is against the poor, against the affluent as it is against the downtrodden, against male as it is female, against white as it is black. Now, as we are all born sinners, think Romans 3:23; we are all also born with different tendencies toward sin. As for addiction, there exists a never-ending variety of options for the potential addict to choose from or perhaps more appropriately, for the Enemy to choose from.

Alcohol serves as the great remover of inhibitions, the socially acceptable chemical that wreaks havoc upon a vast swath of humanity every single day. You can find alcohol everywhere. You can buy alcohol anywhere and an endless variety of alcohol provides just the right option for just about anyone.

An overwhelming quantity of options confronts the traditional beer drinker: domestic, imported, laager, ale, Budweiser, Miller Genuine Draft. Those seeking a little more adventure can delve into the countless types of *harder* alcohol that grace the liquor store shelves from the tamest liqueurs to Evergreen grain alcohol. The more sophisticated may select from among a vast array of wines ranging from the $3 bottle of MD 20/20 to the most expensive bottle of France's finest.

Indeed, the market offers something for everyone and alcohol has become so woven into the fabric of American society that many occasions, situations and circumstances demand alcohol. The sheer absence of any kind of alcohol would surprise many. People just *expect* alcohol to be served.

One would commit an absolute blasphemy not to have a keg at a tailgate party for a football game. A New Year's celebration brings cause for the obligatory bout with champagne. Wedding ceremonies proscribe the traditional toast led by the best man. Old friends come to visit and they will most certainly bring along a six pack of beer or a bottle of wine. Your girlfriend leaves. You grab your buddies and hit the bar to drown your sorrows. Parties, celebrations, ceremonies, events, functions all serve as a seemingly mandatory platform for the consumption of alcohol.

Now to be sure, many probably drink for a lifetime in an entirely responsible manner. Many never get behind the wheel of a car after having one drink, let alone too many. Many will never drink to the point where they behave in a way that they would never otherwise behave, that they would one day regret. Some will remain perfectly under control when consuming alcohol and will *always* know when to say when.

But, there are many who will not, probably more I would contend. A vast array of people, and I would argue the vast majority of consumers, are not always perfectly under control while under the influence of alcohol. As we saw with Ms. Laurel, though alcohol by itself can be very dangerous, it frequently serves as a gateway to other things, sometimes very serious things.

We must remember that Satan is as crafty as he is powerful and he will stop at nothing in leading men to destruction. As such, one who would never smoke marijuana when sober or would never dream of trying cocaine, or crystal meth, or crack when sober, just might if under the influence of alcohol. I've never met an addict who said, "you know, I think I'll start abusing crystal meth today," or, "I think I'll become a crack-head today." More often than not, they got drunk at a party and someone put something in front of them. Nothing more is required as the Scourge takes it from there.

Satan's array of chemical weaponry merely begins with alcohol. Admittedly, these conclusions stem from nothing more than my personal observations. I have drawn my conclusions from experiential research only, admittedly shoddy, but marijuana continues to rise in popularity, particularly among younger people. Almost all teenagers experiment with marijuana or at least are confronted with the option.

Depending upon which part of the country you live in, marijuana may just be more socially acceptable than even alcohol. I had an Army buddy once from Montana who used to smoke marijuana with his parents. No big deal. In fact, as he informed me, they actually looked down upon those who abused alcohol. Colorado recently legalized marijuana and it would seem obvious that other states will soon follow.

Again, drawing from observation, but marijuana acts much like alcohol in that it almost always leads to something else. I've never met an addict whose sole vice was marijuana. I'm sure they exist, but all of the addicts I've met either stuck with alcohol or moved from alcohol and marijuana onto something harder. Maybe you know the kind of thing I'm talking about here.

My family and I lived in rural Kentucky for several years and rural Kentucky addicts loved crystal meth. Once you've seen someone addicted to crystal meth, you'll never forget. It will haunt you. Methamphetamine rots teeth badly, *meth mouth* as it's called. People lose weight, becoming stick-figure thin. They lose their hair. Their eyes become bloodshot. Beauty becomes ugliness. Meth transforms people from normal looking folks into walking corpses in a manner of months. I've never seen the image of God desecrated like I have from the rot of crystal meth abuse. Meth has migrated though. No longer do only white, rural addicts abuse it as it has infiltrated into our urban centers where it competes with crack cocaine for supremacy among the afflicted.

People consume cocaine for the party. People have told me amazing tales of cocaine's ability to juice them up for days at a time. It compels them to great heights. It drives them, mercilessly. Yet, unlike crack or meth, cocaine is expensive, typically thought of as the drug of the affluent though enterprising addicts will invent innumerable ways to obtain their drug of choice.

In most areas, crack cocaine serves as the end of the line. It seems like just about every addict I've known ended up on crack at some point, the final destination, so to speak, the terminal stop. Again, I've never met anyone who woke up desiring to be a crack addict. No one wakes up and says, "I want to be a crack-head." It progresses, assuredly. Crack costs very little. Crack provides an amazingly powerful and an amazingly quick high. Crack addicts nearly instantaneously. Crack is everywhere. Crack destroys. Of course I've left out a litany of other drugs. Heroin springs to mind. Do people still do acid?

You might ask, "Smith, how on earth can you know all of this?" Again, I have done very little research for this work. I didn't need to. I've based these statements solely upon my personal observations and what I've read. An interesting thing has occurred over the last couple of years. The Lord has placed an increasing number of folks in my life that have battled these addictions, folks that are ravaged by addiction.

Growing up, I remember with vivid detail the 'Stoners'. My high school maintained a very strict segregation of social cliques. The jocks didn't really socialize with the nerds and no one socialized with the Stoners. They all wore long hair and denim jackets adorned with black magic marker representations of their favorite heavy metal band. Metallica springs to mind. They existed unto themselves. I don't remember ever even seeing marijuana. That was for the Stoners, not for *normal* people. I just never knew anyone that did drugs, ever.

God has seen fit to change that condition and from those He has introduced to me, their various testimonies, and my own personal observations, it has become very clear to me that Satan has found an amazing tool that is no respecter of person or status. Satan has found a readily available and often highly sought-after tool that has assisted him in the demise of countless thousands, tens of thousands, millions even.

A simple fact strikes me. I live in the Bible Belt, a military town, middle class, a Baptist church on every single corner. I could not believe it when I started discovering that my town has a drug problem. It just wasn't feasible. How could this be? Yet, the more Ami and I became involved in the foster system and the more we got involved in some local ministries, the more it became apparent that the scourge of addiction had beset our town, our city, and this scourge afflicts equally, without prejudice. This scourge is a great equalizer.

Think about the utility of Satan's arsenal with respect to the sheer number of options available. He can bombard one with alcohol, available everywhere, advertised on television, made to seem perfectly cool and enjoyable, maybe even mandatory on some occasions. He can stick with alcohol to destroy and it destroys plenty or he can perhaps use it or possibly marijuana to lower someone's inhibitions enough until someone places another drug, something harder, in front of them.

Each of us has a weakness. Each of us possesses a vulnerability. In drugs and alcohol, Satan has a vast array of tools at his disposal that he will use without hesitation to exploit those weaknesses and they are everywhere. Drugs and alcohol are everywhere. And they are fun or so many pop culture depictions would indicate. The fun though readily dissolves as the addiction takes hold and begins to control the person, to drive the person and eventually to destroy the person.

Chemical addiction is a vast problem, an immense problem, a plague the likes of which humanity has never before experienced. Chemical addiction threatens the very fabric of our nation, the core of our existence. Few exist that are not affected by its influence either directly or indirectly.

I can make all of these statements with total confidence. I urge you to do the research. I challenge you. Perform an internet search for it. How much money does our country spend on 'The War on Drugs'? Millions? Billions? How much does the federal government budget for the Drug Enforcement Agency? The sale of opium, used to make heroin, largely funds our enemy in Afghanistan, the United States' most recent war. Interestingly enough, the world's largest consumer of heroin is, you guessed it, the United States.

Consider the irony. Our enemies are killing our soldiers with weaponry and fighters funded by selling a drug to us that has a similar effect at home, destroying us but on an immensely larger scale. Having been in Afghanistan, I have flown in a helicopter over miles and miles of vast, seemingly endless fields of blooming poppy plants.

How much money does the illegal drug trade yield? Mexican drug cartels wage a violent and nasty insurgency, a war, competing to control drug trafficking and the billions of dollars of profit associated with it. Overmanned and outgunned, the Mexican government desperately wants to stop them. They are beheading people in Mexico over this! How much money do prescription drug sales generate yearly in America? Billions? Trillions? I don't know the answer to all of these, but I've lived long enough to notice a number of different things.

So, while I encourage you to research, I encourage you even more to open your eyes and look around and realize that we are fighting a battle for the soul of humanity and that Satan oppresses and afflicts a generation of people like never before and chemical addiction is the catalyst.

Consider your city. Assess where you live. Consider your friends and family. Do you know an addict? Do you know folks who abuse chemicals? Do you know someone who has made a life-changing decision while under the influence of a chemical? Open your eyes and actually *see*. I think you might be surprised at the grim reality on the street. Drugs and alcohol are truly a great equalizer, a perfect weapon for Satan in his pursuit of the destruction of all nations and all people, his desire to desecrate the very image of God.

Chapter 3 Discussion

READ Romans 2:1-16 and take a time of prayer. In light of this passage:

1) What is Paul's main point concerning sin?

2) Who does he address in verse 1?

3) What does Paul mean in verse 11 when he says, "there is no favoritism with God"?

Read James 2:10, Romans 3:23 and Isaiah 64:6 and take a time of prayer.

4) What is the major thrust of these passages?

5) Are some sins more egregious than others? Does God truly view all sin the same.

In light of this chapter:

6) Do you know someone who struggles with more than one type of chemical addiction?

7) Do you agree with the statement, “Chemical addiction is a vast problem, an immense problem, a plague the likes of which humanity has never before experienced”? Why or why not?

8) Do you personally know someone who has made a life-changing decision while under the influence of drugs and/or alcohol?

Chapter Four

Introducing Dell

DELL speaks as matter-of-factly about his lifetime of drug and alcohol abuse as he does about his newfound passion for making his own hot sauce. On an amazingly beautiful Saturday, crisp and clear, I drove out to his little country home for an interview. Negotiating the winding two lane road for the 30 minute trip, I reflected at length on Dell and his struggle with the demons that had shaped his life from his earliest days.

I still remember the first time that I met Dell. Laurel informed us that she had a new boyfriend. I don't know who was more excited, Laurel or me and Ami. Laurel's husband had left her literally, because she would not drink alcohol or smoke marijuana with him anymore. Clean for many months, she had regained custody of her son — we were his foster parents — and was living, for the first time in as long as she could remember, the way that she knew she should, clean and drug free.

Her husband did not want to change. He had no intentions of leaving behind these things that were destroying their family, but that he had grown accustomed to and comfortable with. So he left, and as much as I love marriage and as much as I hate to see a family break up, I can't help but think it was for the best. Maybe this is the secular world talking.

Then we met Dell. Laurel had gotten a new job at a tile plant and she started work around five in the morning. So we started watching Logan until he got on the school bus. She typically dropped him off around 4:30. One day she announced that her new boyfriend who worked at the same plant would be dropping him off.

I had gotten in the habit of setting my alarm and waiting at the door for Laurel so that her knocking on the door would not wake anyone else up. Well, this particular morning, as I sat waiting, headlights appeared and a truck came tearing down the hill toward our house. As it rounded the corner at the top of the hill, I thought to myself, "Is that Mötley Crüe!?!"

About that time, the truck crested the hill and came to a screeching halt in front of our home blaring loud, 1980's heavy metal music. The door kicked open and a man came to the door hustling Laurel's son along. I opened the door and with a curt, "here he is," I met Dell. He turned brusquely and departed.

From then on, virtually every morning as I waited, myself and my neighbors were treated to an endless assortment of 1980's hair band music. I still laugh about it to this day. As much as my wife and I are children of the 80's - I will sporadically take a trip down memory lane by playing some of my old CD's much to the amusement of my children - I cannot imagine intentionally subjecting myself to that sort of sonic assault at five in the morning!

Yet, Dell turned out to be great for Laurel and he recently proposed to her. He just started driving a concrete truck and they live a joyful existence, both of them having left behind, at least for now, the demons of their addictions. Yet, the fallout from the struggle lingers. The sheer recency of their struggles casts an ever-present pall over everything that they do, fading, but always present.

Dell opened our interview by presenting me a jar of his most recent creation, a hot sauce made from the Trinidad Scorpion Ghost Chili, known as Moruga. This sauce was so hot, Dell informed me, that he literally had to wear gloves, an apron, and a mask while preparing it, which begs the obvious question, "How in the world could one actually consume it!?"

He assured me that it was several million times hotter than a Habañero pepper. I assured him that I wasn't a huge fan of spicy food, so he reached in, found a jar of his "mild" sauce, and offered it to me. I accepted and later, it turned out to be pretty good. Then, sitting at the kitchen table, looking out over a little field on this gorgeous Tennessee fall morning, Dell shared his story with me. I started by asking when he had his first drink of alcohol.

Memphis

DELL grew up in Memphis and around the age of 13, he tried his first drink. His mother provided it for him. She figured that if he wanted to drink, he would, so she wanted to be there, to keep him safe. Dell's parents had divorced when he was much younger and his mom raised him by herself. Dell's dad, an alcoholic, drank constantly and much like his father, Dell liked it from the beginning. He knew, from the very first taste, from the very first time that he put the bottle to his lips, that he liked it. As the sips became swallows and one beer became two, it began to change the way he felt, replacing those intense feelings of insecurity, those feeling of not belonging that plagued Dell consistently.

A few years later, he tried weed. He was hanging out at his friend Richard's house. They tried everything together and just as with alcohol, Dell liked marijuana from the beginning. In alcohol and marijuana, he had found what he had always been looking for. They made him feel normal, not overbearing or high strung. He felt just like everyone else, or at least what he would imagine everyone else felt like. For a kid that never felt like he fit in, never felt normal, it was a welcome feeling.

Memphis is a tough city and it was a tough place to grow up, especially for a skinny white kid. More than many other cities,

Memphis still displays the tendency toward racial segregation and the social ills of a previous era. Dell grew up on the front lines of the racial rift in a predominantly black school and a predominantly black neighborhood. He fought frequently, was teased and bullied, picked on, an outcast. One day in high school, a bunch of kids jumped him, tried to take his jewelry, and this time, Dell fought back. The fight turned into a brawl and the administration felt they had no choice. They expelled Dell. He never returned to school.

Dell showed absolutely no emotion as he described the institutional and familial racism that served as a foundation of his upbringing, underpinning his thoughts and beliefs for as long as he could remember. His dad raised him to hate black people, or any other kind of people for that matter and his circumstances did nothing but reinforce every stereotype.

In Memphis, the black kids knew that they possessed a vast majority and they were not shy in displaying it. This did nothing but reinforce the racist beliefs that had dominated Dell's upbringing. Dell remembered very clearly his Dad even turning off the television if a black person came on. He would not even watch black people on television but interestingly enough, he only watched Alabama football. I wondered how he reconciled the fact that many on the Alabama football team were undoubtedly black.

Dell had exactly one black friend in high school, Collier Harris, but even his presence was fleeting at best. In 1992, a jury convicted Dell's friend of murder and he currently serves 27 years to life. Dell never really had another black friend. I can scarcely imagine how lonely and frustrating his teenage years were.

So Dell sought refuge in the one thing that made him feel like a part of the community, drugs. He did drugs. Inevitably, he began to sell drugs and when he discovered that he could make a significant amount of money with very little effort, he sold more drugs. Gold chains, rings, wads of cash: He had it all, or so it seemed. What did he need school for anyway?

According to Dell, "I don't know what drove me, other than feeling insecure, like I didn't belong. Mom was pretty physically abusive when I was a kid. I'm sure all that stuff had an effect on my psychological upbringing?"

Dell bought his first car at the age of 14, a 1965 Mustang, a classic. He fixed it up, got it running and looking good. Driving gave him the freedom to drink and smoke weed at will, whenever and wherever he wanted and so that's what he did. Every night, he would drift into an alternate reality. Tonight he could be Scarface, selling weed, doing well. He was known, maybe even notorious. It felt good.

Around the age of 17, he started running drugs from Texas to Tennessee and that is when the money really started rolling in. He had started by selling a little marijuana here and there, whatever he had extra. Gradually, this increased to two or three pounds a week when a guy in Texas, a friend of a friend, offered him 100 pounds for $20,000 dollars. Dell took it and sold it and when he saw the profit margin it wasn't long before he was making regular runs between Texas and Memphis.

Another guy in Memphis, a friend, sold cocaine and crack. Before long, Dell was hauling 20 to 30 kilos from Texas along with the marijuana. The thousands of dollars became tens of thousands of dollars. Dell could hardly believe his fortune.

Addicted, Married, Enlisted

SOMEWHERE in the haze of selling and using, Dell got married. At the age of 21, he married his 16 year old girlfriend. She already had a son but that didn't deter either of them. Together, they smoked plenty of weed and drank a lot as well but as Dell put it, the drugs and alcohol hadn't taken over quite yet. In addition to running drugs to and from Texas, he worked for a telecommunications company making decent money. They lived well, comparatively, for several years.

Inevitably though, things began to crumble as they always do. The Scourge is never satiated until it dominates and destroys. One of Dell's frequent and best marijuana customers began trying to hook up with his wife. He had cocaine and she had wanted to try cocaine for some time though Dell had forbid it. In the essence of preserving his marriage, Dell finally gave in and let her.

Before long it became a weekly, then a daily habit, developing into a nasty addiction. Dell soon found himself in the unenviable but not uncommon position of working to support his cocaine habit. He didn't care about bills, the future, he only wanted more cocaine. He started with a gram here and there, but before long, he was doing an 8 ball (3 ½ grams) a day. His marriage continued to unravel along with the rest of his life.

"She was promiscuous to say the least," Dell commented dispassionately on his wife. By this time, they had two children together so they gave treatment a shot in 1998. While in the rehab facility, his wife signed away temporary custody of their two children to her father and stepmother who agreed to return the children once she and Dell completed treatment. They reneged quickly though and told Dell and his wife that they would have to fight to get the kids back.

Somehow though they both finished treatment but they relapsed together just as quickly. Dell decided that they needed to move. They needed a change of scenery and so they packed up everything they owned, which wasn't much, and moved to Dauphin Island in Mobile, Alabama for no particular reason.

He couldn't explain it. They had absolutely no connection with the place. Their kids still lived in Florida with the grandparents. All of Dell's family remained in Memphis. Once there, Dell withdrew into himself, not speaking to anyone for months on end, immersed in the depression and misery of his existence.

They stayed in Mobile for 6 or 7 months and amazingly, didn't use the entire time they were there. Eventually they even decided to fight for custody of their children, which was a Tennessee case. So Dell moved back to Memphis and quickly landed his old job. He had always been a good worker. Dell hired an attorney, initiated the court proceedings, and after a month or two, brought his wife back to Memphis with him. Unfortunately, about a month before court, Dell's wife relapsed.

Her parents had hired a private investigator who documented that she was with numerous other men while Dell traveled out of town for work. Confronted with this, she went to court with no attorney and without Dell's knowledge, and signed away her parental rights. Dell hasn't seen or spoken to his children since. He decided to kill himself. He kicked his wife out and proceeded to smoke crack, eat pills, drink, doing whatever he could to numb the pain of losing his children, losing his wife. Somehow, he continued to live, he just didn't care about anything anymore.

In 2004, Dell began an inevitably abbreviated military career. Perhaps the Army could straighten him out. He had made a new commitment to get sober and surprisingly actually passed the drug test to gain admittance. In 2005, Dell reported to Fort Sill, Oklahoma for basic training. Sixteen weeks later, upon graduation, Dell returned to Memphis a full-fledged member of the National Guard anxious to get started on his new life.

Curiously enough, at some point during this time, he started going to church of all places, met a girl he had known many years ago, and formed a relationship. After a couple of months, they moved in together. For a time, things actually seemed normal, but it was just a matter of time. The façade crumbled quickly. Before long, Dell found himself using again.

His stint in the Army began to unravel just as quickly. Dell started out as a driver but the Army eventually reclassified him as a canon crew member. He doesn't remember driving much and he certainly doesn't remember firing a canon. He does remember that he smoked a lot of weed. They smoked during every weekend drill period behind the motor pool, in the parking lot, wherever they could. Sometimes it seemed like everyone in the National Guard smoked weed.

However, a new commander decided to conduct mandatory and random drug screenings. Knowing he wouldn't pass, Dell informed his chain-of-command and since military policy required it, they sent Dell to rehab for his fourth attempt. He stayed for two and half months at the Memphis Recovery Center, his first contact with Alcoholics Anonymous, got into a fight, and was asked to leave. They simply were not equipped to deal with anger as explosive as Dell's. In April of 2007, Dell refused another drug screen and the Army chaptered him out. He found himself right back where he started, on the streets of Memphis, his military career over, hope fading.

Unraveling

AT this time, the Scourge began to afflict in earnest, to take ahold of his life. Dell bounced from job to job, relapsed over and over until one weekend, his girlfriend went out of town to visit her parents. Dell stole everything he could, sold it all, and set the house on fire. He walked away with a bag of clothes and found himself homeless on the streets in Frayser, Memphis. (Curiously, this happens to be where Dewayne, my oldest son, grew up.)

To say that Dell was drifting at this point would be a vast understatement. He lived nearly off the grid eventually ending up hanging out at a Bar called *Harpo's*. *Harpo's* never closed, ever. It was open 24 hours a day, seven days a week, even on Christmas and New Year's. Dell actually stayed at the bar for four or five months until he met a guy who had an abandoned camper in his back yard where he crashed for another 6 or 7 months. There was no water, no electricity. Dell didn't really have a job to speak of.

Somehow though, he scratched together enough money to buy a trailer in a rundown trailer park. It did have electricity and running water, but that was about it. The floor was full of holes; there were roaches everywhere. "It was nasty," Dell confirmed. He stayed there for about a year until he decided once again to kill himself.

He had reached the apex of his misery, so great was the Scourge. It had run its course. His reasons to live had vanished long ago. Alone in his anguish, death appeared as a respite. He welcomed it.

Sitting there one night, around the middle of June, 2008, Dell decided it was time. He could not possibly continue in the misery of this existence. The only thing he owned, that he hadn't sold to support his drug habit, was his Smith and Wesson .45. So, sitting there, in his nasty living room at seven in the morning — he had been up all night drinking and doing drugs — Dell decided to blow his brains out. God had other ideas, it would seem.

God sent Joel O'Steen. Sitting on the floor of his trailer with his gun to his head and the television on in the background, Dell heard a man speaking. He listened. Dell had no recollection of what the man said, no recollection of the content of any sermon, but as he told me, "something clicked, something changed." He put the gun down and listened.

Following Joel O'Steen, the show *Intervention* came on. Dell picked up his phone and called the number that flashed at the end. Maybe, he didn't want to die after all. They couldn't take him without insurance, but they gave him another number, a lifeline perhaps. They had put him in contact with Buffalo Valley treatment center in Hohenwald, TN and thirteen days later, on July 2, 2008, Dell showed up for treatment.

I am always amazed to see God work and to see the mechanisms He uses, the people, the circumstances. As Dell told me his story, I was in awe that literally, a Joel O'Steen sermon had saved him. Rather, God chose to save him through a Joel

O'Steen sermon. I serve a very conservative, reformed Southern Baptist church. Most serious students of the Word that I know consider Joel O'Steen somewhat of a theological featherweight, perhaps even a prosperity gospel preacher, even a false prophet. So you can imagine my surprise when Dell relayed this to me. I was blown away and instantly thought of Isaiah 10:5-7:

> Woe to Assyria, the rod of My anger — the staff in their hands is My wrath. I will send him against a godless nation; I will command him to go against a people destined for My rage, to take spoils, to plunder, and to trample them down like clay in the streets. But this is not what he intends; this is not what he plans. It is his intent to destroy and to cut off many nations.

God used the nation of Assyria to judge Israel, to destroy the Northern Kingdom as Israel had drifted further and further from God despite repeated warnings from the prophets. Yet, Assyria did not seek to serve God in their conquest. Assyria, an evil nation, intended only to plunder, to murder, to destroy.

The theology here speaks to *compatibility*, to God using the actual intentions of man, evil intentions even, to accomplish His will. In that same spirit, Dell heard from Joel O'Steen and decided not to kill himself. No matter what you think of Joel O'Steen's theology, Dell would clearly argue that God had used him in the mightiest of ways, to save his very life.

From 2000 to 2008, Dell had lived an out of control existence. As he explained:

> I'd steal anything that wasn't tied down, rob you, especially when I was homeless. You know, I'd just hit 'em, knock 'em out, steal their stuff, at gunpoint sometimes. I'd get them coming out of their car at the grocery store.
>
> I shot a couple of people. I ran over two people with a

> car. I did anything, to change how I felt. I wanted to feel the adrenaline rush, getting away with robbing people did it for me. There was this feeling of power, feeling of superiority over another person. This drove me to do a lot of things. The drugs made it that much worse.

But here he was, back in treatment:

> At every other treatment center, I didn't feel like I belonged. I felt uncomfortable. I developed an ability to make people hate me. I guess this was my way of being in control of how people felt about me.
>
> As I kid, I had always been really insecure. Instead of wondering how you felt, now, I would make you hate me just to be certain of how you felt. I didn't realize what I was doing until later, looking back. I always had to be in control.

A Last Gasp

DELL noticed a difference from the beginning at Buffalo Valley. They made Dell feel welcome, like he belonged, even though he was mean, hateful, insecure. They made him feel like one of them. This had a huge impact on him. He stayed for 28 days but he knew, Dell knew, that it wasn't long enough. He needed more time and so he prayed. He prayed that he could get more time. He wasn't ready. Two days prior to release, the case manager called and told him that she had a yearlong program in Clarksville, TN if he was interested. Dell, clinging to hope, said yes.

However, Dell's previous existence and transgressions would not so easily be left behind. After 19 days in Clarksville, his Probation Officer called from Memphis telling him to return to Memphis, turn himself in, and submit to a transfer back to Memphis to account for previous offenses. On August 20th, he left treatment, returned to Memphis, and ended up not leaving jail until December of that year when he was remanded to the Shelby County penal farm to serve out the remainder of his sentence. But he was sober, for the first time in years, he was sober.

Eventually he got out of jail and returned to Clarksville. Buffalo Valley had saved him a bed and Dell stayed for 14 months. He got a job at Rainbow Tile, where he met Laurel, and got an apartment. Dell worked. He was clean, for the first time, and so he worked and he worked. Furiously. He had accumulated an ocean of debt. His credit score was an abysmal 430 and so for nearly two years, he worked, 80 hours a week, sometimes more. He paid debts. He paid loans he didn't know he had. Gradually, he dug his way out.

He even applied for a loan and bought a small house in the country. As soon as he saw the house, he knew he had to have it. Thirty days later, he moved in. He couldn't believe what was happening, how his life had turned around.

Dell's last drink had been July 1st, 2008. He got drunk, went to a strip club, and spent the money that he was supposed to use to get to treatment the next day. He had to actually borrow money to get to treatment. He ran out of gas on the way, in Jackson, Tennessee, and walked 5 miles from a rest area to the nearest Western Union where he called his mom. She wired him a few dollars so he could buy a gas can and make it to Clarksville.

On July 2nd, 2008, Dell had begun his journey into life, into sobriety but it wasn't without its toll. Having been abused all those years, his body had taken a terrible beating requiring two surgeries. He had ruptured discs in his neck, a destroyed shoulder but he considered himself lucky just to be alive. Sobriety hasn't been easy though.

> Dealing with people is the hardest thing, living everyday normal life with nothing else to cope with it,

> dealing with the stuff that normal people do. I always dealt with it with drugs or a drink or something like that. I'd always been really insecure, never felt like I was a part of anything, always an outcast. I didn't' belong anywhere, and so now, I'm learning how to accept who I am without drugs and alcohol, just being me … that's the hardest thing there is.

Dell delivered this with a decisive hit of his coffee. I asked him, "What would you tell someone else who struggles?"

"There is hope, there is a better way," he responded.

> Buffalo Valley was where I connected to a higher power. They provided a safe place for me to be, without temptation. I got connected to a higher power and began to research Native American culture and belief systems. My mom's family is Native American and it made the most sense to me. I had faith in something other than myself. I found some hope.
>
> Other people that I saw that had recovered, they helped me see that maybe it was possible. I can't knock anybody else for what they believe or what religious background they have. If Christianity is the youngest form of religion, how are the millions of people who were here before that wrong?
>
> I believe that there is a God and it's not me … God is that spirit that gives life to everything, not birds, animals, or plants. God is that force that gives life to everything … Helped me to stay focused on what I wanted … hope that I could have a better life. I never felt like I deserved a better life with the way that I treated people. I felt like a complete piece of garbage.

At the AA meetings my family and I attended in support of Laurel, I observed firsthand how active Dell had become in the program. He became a leader. Dell felt immensely rewarded, satisfied, being sober and seeing people go through the same struggle, seeing the lights come on.

Reflections

A newly sober person is hopeless and depressed, frequently suicidal. Dell continues to find great joy in seeing the change, pondering his own dramatic journey through the gauntlet of addiction.

> In my struggle with drugs and alcohol, nothing was sufficient enough to make me want to change. I didn't have the ability to change. When I lost my children, the most important thing I could think of, it was not important enough to stop. I loved drugs more than anything else in the world. I didn't realize it, but the drugs told me where to go and what to do. They were in complete control of every thought. If I wasn't drinking and doing drugs, I was thinking about drinking and drugging, until the higher power, until I prayed for him to take my obsession away.
>
> There was no hope for me in anything. I absolutely believe it takes an act of God, an act of providence, something bigger than me to make somebody want to change, to take that away with sufficient force to get sober and stay sober.
>
> Even my children weren't enough to stop me. When the God that I pray to saw that I was ready, he put people in my life, but not until I was broken and desperate enough, desperate enough to seek help outside this world I guess.

Dell's father died in 2003. His Mom called one day, out of the blue, and simply said, "your Dad died," just like that. Dell had missed the funeral. Yet, Dell's mom had never let go, after all of those years. She stuck by Dell, no matter what he did, as only a mother can.

Dell robbed her. He emptied her bank account on more than one occasion. Yet, she never let go, all the way up until she wired him the money to get to Buffalo Valley that fateful day in 2008. She still lives in the same house in Memphis that he grew up in and has owned her own beauty salon for 38 years. Dealing with her own demons and addictions, after 30 years Dell's mom just quit. There was no program, no rehab, and no treatment. She just quit.

Last year, Dell returned to Memphis, this time to get his Commercial Driver's License. His past still haunted him though as he first had to reconcile his 57 moving violations. He had reckless driving tickets, drag racing, and reckless endangerment. The state had suspended his license a stunning 17 times. The irony of this overpowers me and I'm sure there is great humor here somewhere in the fact that even with this record, Dell became a professional driver obtaining his class A CDL with hazmat endorsement. Dell himself can hardly believe how his life has changed. As he reflected upon the struggle, our conversation turned toward matters of faith.

Interestingly, Dell used a lot of language to describe his journey that sounded like it was transposed right from a Christian systematic theology. He spoke of his own helplessness apart from God, his own inability and powerlessness in the face of the chemical oppression he had endured. He spoke of the sovereignty of God, his own place in the grand plan of God. He spoke of his need for salvation, though admittedly, his concept of salvation was a paradigm shift away from the Christian understanding of this need, this burden. The chasm, the gulf, was ever present.

I asked him about Jesus Christ and we talked for quite some time. Dell, unlike many who are outright hostile toward things of Christ, was quite open to discussing His existence. He had many questions that in his mind, begged the actual feasibility of Christianity. Dell was fine with his life now, how things were, his lot. He had no need for Jesus.

He questioned the age of the universe, the existence of multiple other religions, many predating Christianity. He examined the possibility that aliens brought life to the planet citing the pyramids and amazing linguistic discoveries as possible "proof" that such a condition developing on its own was a narrow possibility. He believed in the spiritual, though he had no concrete explanation for its existence or substance. He was fine with that. It was a fascinating conversation and I did have an opportunity to share the Gospel with him after which I asked him if he wanted to repent of his sin and confess Jesus Christ. He politely declined and we continued with the conversation.

I asked him about prescription meds which he'd never really gotten into. I have become increasingly aware that prescription drug abuse is equally as devastating as any illegal drug abuse.

As he explained it, Dell had always been an upper kind of guy. Pills are downers. He wanted adrenaline, a rush, anything that would give him that feeling. Now he gets a rush from living his life with Laurel, they are engaged and preparing for the future together. Just as when he was drinking and drugging and couldn't imagine living any other way, now he couldn't imagine living the way he had previously. I am honored to consider Dell my friend and I was honored to hear him share his struggle.

I've considered frequently how I might have acted, were I similarly afflicted. Would I have the strength to actually persevere in circumstances similar to Dell's? The struggle's bitter and vicious nature never strays far from my mind.

CHAPTER 4 DISCUSSION

READ Psalm 139:1-16. In light of this passage:

1) What is David's main point of this Psalm?

2) What do verses 13-14 indicate? Compare this with Psalm 8:3-8, also a Davidic Psalm. What is David's point concerning humanity? How does this account for sin?

3) What are the implications of verse 16 for daily living?

In light of this chapter:

4) Where do you see the sovereignty of God manifest itself in Dell's life?

How would you answer Dell's objections to Christianity:

> 5) If Christianity is the youngest form of religion, how are the millions of people who were here before that wrong?
>
> 6) What about the age of the universe?
>
> 7) What about the possibility of life on other planets?

How would you answer the following statement from Dell:

> I believe that there is a God and it's not me ... God is that spirit that gives life to everything, not birds, animals, or plants. God is that force that gives life to everything.

CHAPTER FIVE

Quia Non est Veritas in Vino (There is no truth in wine)

IS drinking alcohol a sin? What say you?

I know of only a few other topics that will get folks, Christians, involved in a heated exchanged. Allow me to lay it out, right up front. Drinking is a sin *for me*. I am a called preacher of the Word of God, a servant of the Lord Jesus Christ and I do not want anything controlling my thoughts and actions except the Holy Spirit. I certainly do not want alcohol controlling my thoughts and actions, as it had been wont to do for a number of years prior to Jesus Christ saving my soul.

Ami and I had a really funny conversation with our preacher once. A bit of testimony here, but in January of 2005, the Lord convicted me to take my family to church. At the time, I didn't recognize or discern the Lord's conviction for I was not a believer, but I felt compelled to get my family in church for the moral training that it would give to our children.

As our oldest daughter entered her teenage years, she became increasingly interested in members of the opposite sex, as teenage girls are prone to do. I looked for any ally I could find as she was turning into a beautiful young lady and the wolves were already starting to circle.

So, we went to a friend's church and I can't tell you how incredibly uncomfortable it felt. I squirmed in my seat. In the church that I grew up attending, you never had to be singled out in any way. You sat down and stood up on cue. You spoke the right words on cue and you submitted to the system. Once you were confirmed and baptized, you were good to go. At least, I thought I was good to go.

Well, we go to this church and it is small, probably less than 20 people and we are obviously the only new people there and they obviously are not used to visitors and so they single us out.

Strike one.

They also didn't have a preacher so an Elder, whatever that was, talked some about the Bible, not really too coherently from what I recall.

Strike two.

And for music, some squirrelly guy with a guitar sang some squirrelly songs about Jesus. No organ. No hymnal.

Strike three!

We were outta there! I still remember on the way out saying to Ami, "I really didn't get much out of that!" Amazing how perspectives change!

Well, Ami's friend at work heard we were looking for a church, so she invited us to hers, Hilldale Baptist, the first Southern Baptist church I had ever attended. The place was absolutely huge. My head spun with all of commotion of people hurrying to and fro. Two, I had never heard preaching like I heard there, from what I recall. Here, for the first time I heard the Gospel message, uncut, in its full power, with all of its teeth, the good, the bad, and the ugly, delivered straightforward, right from the Bible. It absolutely blew me away.

We walked in for the first time and a little old lady named Ms. Mary Parchman immediately recognized that we were visitors and grabbed ahold of us and had us sit right down with her. She remains a great friend of ours to this day.

For the next several weeks, the preacher, Brother Larry, preached directly to me and to my wife, though he did not seem to know that he was preaching straight to me and my wife. As gifted of a preacher as there is, Dr. Larry Robertson has been preaching since he was 15 and he preached with power and authority and as I said, it blew me away. It also blew me away that he was preaching to me.

I had lots of questions and Ami and I would have a discussion that week. *What about baptism? What is this salvation, being born again, thing?* Then that week, Brother Larry would preach on what we had discussed. It got to the point where we were driving home from church and I looked at Ami and she looked at me and we were like, "What is going on here?"

To make a long story short, I eventually ended up being saved at the Passion Play in April 2005 and then made it public at the invitation the following week. To say that the Lord got into my family's life and turned it upside down would be an understatement. I remember at one point months later, as God took hold of more and more of our life, yelling in exasperation and frustration at Ami, "*It can't all be about God can it!?!*"

God thought differently. He is not, it seems, without a sense of irony or maybe even a sense of humor.

I tell you all of that to tell you that Ami and I used to drink, party hard, both of us and as the Lord was drawing us to him, we both began to worry about it. Hilldale Baptist had their member's creed hanging on the wall and it mentioned not drinking. *Were they serious about that?*

So we met with Brother Larry to ask him a bunch of questions, but what we really wanted to know was, could we join the church and still drink. To this day, I still remember the grin on his face as we asked him that question. Here we were, contemplating questions of an eternal nature, our everlasting souls hanging in the balance, and what we wanted to know was, could we still drink? I'm sure that God was smiling at that one.

In Scriptura Veritas (Truth is Scripture)

WHAT does the Bible say? As we sort through the Bible's stance on alcohol, remember the maxim, *interpret Scripture with Scripture*. We'll check what some individual verses say, but remember to interpret them in light of each other and though we'll focus on some narrow issues, try and see a broader context. Let's start with an easy one.

The Bible condemns drunkenness. You will hear Christians on both sides of the fence when it comes to drinking, but as far as drunkenness, the Bible speaks very clearly.

> Wine is a mocker, beer is
> a brawler,
> and whoever staggers
> because of them is not wise.
>
> Proverbs 20:1n

> Don't associate with those
> who drink too much wine,
> or with those who gorge themselves
> on meat.
> For the drunkard and the glutton
> will become poor,
> and grogginess will clothe them in rags.
>
> Proverbs 23:20-21

Note that the Proverb here mentions drunkenness in the same breath and context as gluttony. Also note that the passage from Proverbs 20 makes a general statement about alcohol, *Wine is a mocker, beer is a brawler*. It adds the qualifier "and" not "because" meaning that the first part of the clause does not depend upon the second. The two statements about beer and wine stand alone. Being a mocker and a brawler are clearly not good things. So this passage actually makes a general commentary on alcohol before applying it to drunkenness but, we'll start by focusing on drunkenness and Proverbs 23 definitively condemns drunkenness.

Yeah, but that's the Old Testament. What about the New Testament? As it turns out, Jesus himself addresses drunkenness:

> Be on your guard, so that your minds are not dulled from carousing, drunkenness, and worries of life ...
>
> Luke 21:34a

as does Paul in several places:

> Let us walk with decency, as in the daylight: not in carousing and drunkenness; not in sexual impurity and promiscuity; not in quarreling and jealousy.
>
> Romans 13:13

> But now I am writing you not to associate with anyone who bears the name of brother who is sexually immoral or greedy, an idolater or a reviler, a drunkard or a swindler. Do not even eat with such a person.
>
> 1 Corinthians 5:11

> Now the works of the flesh are obvious: sexual immorality, moral impurity, promiscuity, idolatry, sorcery, hatreds, strife, jealousy, outbursts of anger, selfish ambitions, dissensions, factions, envy, drunkenness, carousing, and anything similar ...
>
> Galatians 5:19-21

> And don't get drunk with wine, which leads to reckless actions, but be filled with the Spirit:
>
> Ephesians 5:18

and the Apostle Peter as well:

> For there has already been enough time spent in doing the will of the pagans: carrying on in unrestrained behavior, evil desires, drunkenness, orgies, carousing, and lawless idolatry.
>
> 1 Peter 4:3

The Bible speaks very clearly on the subject. Notice the language and associations that Paul and Peter use to describe drunkenness. They describe drunkenness as "the will of the pagans", mentioning it in the same breath as *orgies, carousing, sexual immorality, promiscuity, jealousy* amongst other things.

Notice too that the Apostles are quick to point out that they are speaking to *brothers*, fellow Christians. Pagans behave in this manner, getting drunk, not those of Christ.

Jesus warns against the dulling of the mind due to drunkenness. Paul speaks to the control of the Spirit as opposed to reckless actions caused by drunkenness. Clearly, Biblically speaking, a Christian should not get drunk. It does not get much more cut and dried than that, from the Proverbs, from the mouth of Jesus, from two of the greatest Apostles.

Furthermore, the Bible clearly addresses those who are to be leaders in the church. James, the brother of Jesus, makes a general statement concerning leader or teachers in the church:

> Not many should become teachers, my brothers, knowing that we will receive a stricter judgment; for we all stumble in many ways.
>
> James 3:1

James speaks to the higher standard that teachers and leaders will be held. Paul likewise comments specifically to this higher standard:

> An overseer, therefore, must be above reproach, the husband of one wife, self-controlled, sensible, respectable, hospitable, an able teacher, <u>not addicted to wine</u>, not a bully but gentle, not quarrelsome, not greedy ...
>
> 1 Timothy 3:3

> For an overseer, as God's manager, must be blameless, not arrogant, not quick tempered, <u>not addicted to wine</u>, not a bully, not greedy for money,
>
> Titus 1:7

Paul speaks to leadership as an ordained and divine function. A leader in the church serves as "God's manager". God ordains godly leaders for the church and God gives the leader stewardship over the led. God requires these qualifications of His chosen leaders and of all the qualities that Paul could address, he states that the leader may not be addicted to wine. The higher standard of leadership in the church does not include addiction. Yeah, but may a leader drink? What if he doesn't get drunk? We'll address that shortly.

The earliest note of caution comes from the book of Numbers whereby God, through Moses, addresses those who want to make a special vow, called the Nazarite vow. The Nazarite vow is a special vow of holiness and purity containing special grooming and sacrificial practices. For the one making the vow, the purpose of the vow is "to consecrate himself to the LORD". (Num. 6:2) To do this, "he is to abstain from wine and beer". Moses goes on to say, "He must not drink vinegar made from wine or from beer." (verse 6:3a) Additionally, he also mentions, "He must not drink any grape juice or eat fresh grapes or raisins." (verse 6:3b)

Here we have a man or woman looking to consecrate themselves to the LORD, looking to set themselves aside in a special way, and God instructs them to not drink wine and beer. Not only that, don't drink any grape juice, or eat any grapes or raisins or don't eat anything from the grapevine, seeds, skin, anything.

Does that nullify or diminish the initial command not to drink wine or beer or does God say, not only don't drink wine and beer, but I don't even want you to have anything to do with the plant from which wine comes. This would be akin to commanding someone, "Don't hang out in a bar and not only that, don't even drive on the street that the bar is on or wear your favorite t-shirt that you got at the bar."

Clearly God considers the Nazarite vow a next level vow of holiness and dedication, free not only from alcohol, but from the actual sources of alcohol as well. An astute reader must ask the question, "Why would God consider abstinence from alcohol a prerequisite for holiness?"

Let's spend a few minutes checking out the first part of Proverbs 31.

> Don't spend your energy
> on women
> or your efforts on those
> who destroy kings.
>
> It is not for kings, Lemuel,
> it is not for kings
> to drink wine
> or for rulers to desire beer.
>
> Otherwise, they will drink,
> forget what is decreed,
> and pervert justice for all
> the oppressed.
>
> Give beer to one who is dying,
> And wine to one whose life
> is bitter.
>
> Let him drink so that
> he can forget his poverty

and remember his trouble
no more.

Proverbs 31:3-7

We could spend a lot of time camping out on this Proverb. At first glance, the non-discerning biblical scholar would look at verse 6 and say, "Look, the Bible commands me to give beer and wine to those who are dying and those with bitter lives so that they can forget their poverty and trouble!"

Wine and beer must be good then! They help the dying and bitter to forget their poverty and trouble. Yet, let's take it in the context. In this oracle from a mother to a son, the king, she says in essence, "Act like a king, Lemuel.

"Don't chase women or spend time with those who will tear you down. That kind of thing is beneath you as a king just like wine and beer. That is not for you. The effects are bad. What if you get drunk and forget what has already been decided and betray justice."

In other words, "You are better than that, Lemuel.

"Beer and wine are for the dying because it doesn't matter if they are drunk or drinking, for they will soon be dead."

One would error greatly to say that Proverbs 31 promotes alcohol abuse for the downtrodden. Rather, the mother encourages her son the king to be better than that, to be above this kind of practice. As disciples of the King, we would all do well to seek royal and kingly advice and wisdom. As followers of the King, we should seek to emulate the King's practices, and in Proverb 31, the Word mentions the practice of drinking beer and wine as being a lesser practice.

Again, the Proverb does not expressly condemn alcohol consumption for everyone, but it certainly puts some meat to the skeleton as to the biblical stance on consumption.

Isaiah speaks to the consumption of alcohol:

Woe to those who rise early
in the morning
in pursuit of beer,
who linger into the evening,
inflamed by wine.

Isaiah 5:11

Woe to those who are heroes
at drinking wine,
who are fearless at mixing beer ...

Isaiah 5:22a

Isaiah speaks these words in the middle of a very metaphorically-laden exposition against Israel and their unfaithfulness to God so he certainly speaks in allegory. Yet, I find it interesting that of all the activities Isaiah could have picked to describe those straying from God, in these two verses, he picked alcohol use. In many other passages, he describes it as prostitution. Interesting.

In Luke chapter one, the priests choose Zechariah by lot to enter the sanctuary of the Lord and burn incense, as was the custom. As the assembly prays outside the sanctuary, an angel of the Lord appears before Zechariah and says to him:

Do not be afraid, Zechariah,
because your prayer
has been heard.

Your wife Elizabeth will bear you
a son,
and you will name him John.

There will be joy and delight
for you,
and many will rejoice
at his birth.

For he will be great in the sight
of the Lord

and will never drink wine
or beer.

He will be filled
with the Holy Spirit
while still
in his mother's womb.

Luke 1:13-15

Did you catch that? The angel of the Lord prophesies to Zechariah the priest about his future son, John the Baptist, who, in the words of Jesus Himself, was the greatest of all of the prophets. "I assure you: Among those born of women no one greater than John the Baptist has appeared." (Matthew 11:11a) The angel says that, "He will be great in the sight of the Lord" *and* he, "will never drink wine or beer." On the contrary, "He will be filled with the Holy Spirit" from his existence in his mother's womb.

The wording does not indicate a causal relationship between NOT drinking wine or beer and being great in the sight of the Lord but they do seem to indicate exclusive notions. That is, John will be great not because he will never drink wine or beer but he will be great *and* in line with being great in the sight of the Lord, he will never drink wine or beer.

The causality, though not definitive, permeates the relationship. As interesting as it is that Isaiah utilizes drinking to describe spiritual adultery, much like using prostitution, as interesting as it is that the Nazirite vow requires one to refrain not only from alcohol, but from all aspects of the plant from which alcohol comes, it is equally as interesting here that the prophesy immediately following the declaration of John's greatness is that he will never drink wine or beer followed immediately by the fact that he will be filled with the Holy Spirit from the womb.

Again, these seem to be contradictory or exclusive notions. John will be great. He will not drink. He will be filled with the

Holy Spirit. Though the relationship between the ideas lacks a definitive causality, one can certainly derive an aspect of exclusivity quite easily.

Though it does not condemn mere consumption outright, Scripture does frequently mention it as an issue. Scripture condemns drunkenness. God holds teachers and leaders to a higher a standard and as such, drunkenness disqualifies one from the role or position. Kings should adhere to a higher standard than to consume alcohol. Scripture frequently mentions consumption in contrast to notions such as greatness, holiness, and being filled with the Holy Spirit. Clearly, Scripture speaks to issues with alcohol consumption.

Yet to be fair, God made all things and he pronounced them good. He did.

> He causes grass to grow
> For the livestock
> and provides crops
> for man to cultivate,
> producing food
> from the earth,
> wine that makes
> man's heart glad —
> making his face shine with oil —
> and bread that sustains man's heart.
> Proverbs 104:14-15

Proverbs 104 describes wine as something that makes a man's heart glad, makes his face shine with oil, which we can presume to be a good thing. Besides, in John chapter 2, at a wedding in Cana, Jesus turns water into wine, his first recorded miracle. Perhaps the Bible only condemns drunkenness and not *mere* consumption. I mean, if Jesus made it and the Proverbs declares that ultimately, God made it, then it cannot possibly be bad, right.

Scholars debate the different meanings of the words for wine and beer in the Old Testament, defining them as "strong drink" in some places or implying that they refer to non-fermented, nonalcoholic, drink, grape juice in effect.

I've heard all of these and I don't intend to provide a detailed exegesis on the different words for wine and beer and alcoholic drink in the Old Testament. I don't believe it necessary. Let's take a look at the words of Jesus.

> For John did not come eating or drinking, and they say, "He has a demon!" the Son of Man came eating and drinking and they say, "Look, a glutton and a drunkard, a friend of tax collectors and sinners!" Yet wisdom is vindicated by her deeds.
>
> Matthew 11:18-19

The religious leaders of the day are accusing Jesus of being a drunkard. Logically, they would probably not accuse him of this if he did not actually consume wine with actual alcohol in it. In fact, this accusation makes it likely that Jesus consumed wine, fermented wine, wine with alcohol in it. I mean, Jesus actually turned quite a bit of water into wine at the wedding in Cana as recorded in the book of John. Certainly this was actual wine, not some sort of grape juice, as all of the guests partook and the master of the feast even commented on the quality of the wine that had been provided.

Yet, I cannot help but think that 1st century Palestinians did not exactly have easy access to drinking water. You could not turn on the water in the kitchen or hit the store for a bottle of Gatorade. Wine was probably something they had to drink and I am assuming that wine kept better than water and I am also going to make an assumption that their 1st century technology did not brew wine with the same alcoholic content as our modern processes produce today.

Again, I am clearly speculating. I can honestly think of a valid counterargument. West Virginia moonshiners produce some of the most potent stuff alive, so I'm told, deep in the Appalachian Mountains, far from any sort of modern technology, under very primitive conditions.

Immolatis Simulacrorum (Sacrificed to Idols)

LET me tell how God pushed me over the edge on the issue. Let's be honest, alcohol is not actually evil. When and if I speak to it as being evil, I flirt with hyperbole, allegory. Alcohol is actually an inanimate object. It is amoral.

It doesn't have a morality. Paul addresses a similar issue in 1 Corinthians 8. In the pagan temples, after the priests had sacrificed the animal to the idol, they would take the meat to the back of the temple and sell it to anyone who wanted to buy it. Nothing magical, just food. Paul comments to the practice of whether a Christian should buy such meat or not.

> About eating food offered to idols, then, we know that an "idol is nothing in the world," and that "there is no God but one." For even if there are so-called gods, whether in heaven or on earth — as there are many "gods" and many "lords" —
>
> 1 Corinthians 8:4-5

Paul acknowledges the amorality of such meat. We know that no other gods exist, only the one true God, and that meat sacrificed to these false gods, to these idols, is just meat. He continue:

> However, not everyone has this knowledge. In fact, some have been so used to idolatry up until now, that when they eat food offered to an idol, their conscience, being weak, is defiled. Food will not make us acceptable to God. We are not inferior if we don't eat, and we are not better if we do eat. But be careful that this right of yours in way becomes a stumbling block to the weak. Then the weak person, the brother for whom Christ died, is ruined by your knowledge. Now when you sin like this against the brothers and wound their weak conscience, you are sinning against Christ.
>
> 1 Corinthians 8:7-12

You have the right to eat this meat, Paul tells the Corinthians, but in Christianity, you are not the focus. The two greatest commandments tell us to love God and love others as ourselves and to prop up our Christian brothers and sisters, to support them and encourage them in their weaknesses and vulnerabilities. You may need the same someday.

So, Corinthians, many do not understand that God exists as one and many spent their whole lives eating this meat as a sacrifice to idols, to false gods, and if they see you, a fellow Christian, partaking, then they may make the wrong assumption, that you eat to the idols as well. This may thereby damage their faith and as Paul points out, when you sin like this against your brothers in Christ, *you are sinning against Christ*! Paul's words are fairly damning.

Let's make the hermeneutical leap. If Scripture does not outright condemn alcohol consumption, it certainly requires much care in handling it. Scripture speaks to consumption as an issue. Scripture speaks to the danger of consumption. Though the Bible may not expressly prohibit me, a Christian, from having a beer while out to dinner with my wife, what if a new Christian walks in and sees me drinking and doesn't yet fully understand Scripture and why I am drinking, so it must be okay. Am I being a stumbling block for him? Am I damaging the faith of a weaker brother? If so, then *I am sinning against Christ!*

The more I thought about his one and God's call to sanctification, to be set apart from the world, the more out of place a glass of beer began to seem in my hand. God calls Christians to holiness, to purity. Now, I drank alcohol for some time after my conversion, but it receded. It waned over time.

The Spirit convicted my wife first. She had started drinking a glass of wine while in the bathtub every night. The glass of wine became two glasses and then three and then she felt the conviction of the Holy Spirit and quit, cold-turkey and in support, I quit with her. My last two beers were at a microbrewery in Nashville in the spring of 2006 and they were glorious! But I don't regret for one second our decision to quit.

I'll still concede that the Bible does not speak entirely black and white on the issue of drinking though I do believe it speaks much more black and white than we would ever care to admit. In my mind though, the most damning biblical evidence against drinking would be:

> Whatever you do, do it enthusiastically [lit. from the soul] as something done for the Lord and not for men …
>
> Colossians 3:16a

Paul tells us that whatever we do, *whatever*, we should do it as something done for the Lord. Now, if you can honestly tell me as you hold that shot of tequila up to your mouth you could look heavenward and proclaim, *O' Father, unto Your Spirit I commend this drink of Tequila*, then go right ahead, but I believe you are fooling yourself. Now don't forget, I used to drink, a lot, and I never observed anyone, even in retrospect, that could have been drinking for the Lord though I guess it is theoretically possible.

Yet, I would like to ask one of my newfound addicted friends what their thoughts are on alcohol. Nobody, nobody wakes up and says, *I think I'll become an alcoholic*. No one wakes up and thinks, *I'll think I'll make a life-changing decision today while under the influence of alcohol*. That's not how it happens, but do you know, as an Army officer, how many young men I've had stand in front of my desk who did exactly that, made a life-changing decision while under the influence of alcohol.

Et Non Est Bonum (Nothing Good)

I can assure you that in the ranks of young men of which the Army is primarily composed, alcohol abuse catalyzes an epidemic, an epidemic of self-destructive behavior fueled by alcohol. I have had 22 to 23 year old kids require 30 day inpatient rehabilitation. 22 to 23 years old! I had one young man who went to rehab, did okay for a little while, decided to start drinking again and declared that he wasn't going to stop because he liked it, on his way out of the Army.

I had another young man get arrested while passed out in a car. He was a good Soldier or so we thought, so we went to bat for him and he actually got a second chance from the Commanding General, a very unusual gift as we had made a persuasive case for leniency. A short time later, he got an actual DUI and while undergoing counseling, as we were doing the paperwork to kick him out of the Army, he got another. Unbelievable.

The first young man to come to the Clarksville Covenant House, me and Ami's ministry for ex-foster kids, suffered from the fallout of two separate DUI convictions. Broke, homeless, with no car, no job, no license and several years of probation and thousands of dollars in fines, he came to us destitute. Just now, several years later, he sees the light at the end of the tunnel though he continues to battle in overcoming the results of the choices he made while under the influence of alcohol.

Young men self-destruct by the thousands while under the influence of alcohol and I have had a front-row seat for much of its aftermath. I can tell you that in addition to getting DUI's, young Soldiers commit domestic violence, quite often fueled by alcohol. Soldier gets drunk. Soldier gets in argument with wife. Soldiers hits wife. Soldier gets arrested. Soldier's career ends and often his marriage as well. Bar fights, drunk and disorderly, drunk in public, manslaughter, I've seen it all and almost always, alcohol was the fuel.

Sexual violence wreaks havoc in the military, some of the vilest crimes you can imagine. A young Soldier raped another young female Soldier while she was passed out drunk. Another young Soldier was offended that his drunken sexual advances were rebuffed and so he held the girl down and masturbated on her. Another young Soldier got drunk and sodomized his wife against her will. Almost always, even in the rudimentary cases of sexual assault — if there is such a thing — alcohol serves as the fuel, the catalyst.

We had a Soldier leave a party drunk and ball up his car on the side of the road, killing himself. The police arrived and observed empty beer cans strewn everywhere, in the car, on the road. As he lay dying, the hospital recorded his blood alcohol content as well over the legal limit. He died and because he was drunk, it initially looked like he would be found NOT in the line of duty thereby negating any benefits his wife and small children would have received. They lost their husband and daddy and would get no money to take care of them, because he was drunk.

Now fortunately a sympathetic police officer and commanders were able to get him found IN the line of duty so that his wife would not have to pay the consequences for his reckless abandon. Yet, as it happened initially, she wouldn't have gotten anything, not even any money to bury him.

Soldiers commit suicide at a record pace, more than one every two days and almost all of them involve some form of substance abuse, primarily alcohol.

A drunk driver killed my uncle, my mother's brother, on Christmas Eve of all days, as he drove home from work to be with his family. The drunk swerved across the center line and hit him head on, killing my Uncle Sam instantly. I bet that you know someone who has been killed by a drunk driver or a family that has been decimated by a drunk driver. I bet you know someone whose life has been destroyed from alcohol consumption or even alcohol addiction. I imagine you know someone who loves someone whose life is being destroyed by alcohol abuse.

As I conceded earlier, some may always maintain self-control while consuming alcohol. Some may never have lost a measure of control of their actions and thoughts and emotions while consuming alcohol. When I used to drink though, I never knew anyone who drank who didn't drink until they at least had a buzz on occasion. I mean, I knew some light drinkers, but even they drank until they felt *some* effects.

Maybe some do maintain control, always but I would bet a year's salary though that for every one of those theoretical people, there are more than a 100 who do not maintain 100% control every single time they drink. How many babies have been conceived out of a drunken encounter? How many babies have been aborted after being accidentally conceived during a drunken encounter?

Alcohol controls people. It controls the mind, the heart, the body. Where do you draw the line? When do you cross the line? One drink? Two? When does the alcohol begin to supplant your control? If you are a Christian, when does the alcohol supplant the Holy Spirit in guiding and controlling your thoughts, feelings, and actions? Have you ever met anyone who said, *you know, I'm really glad I started drinking back in the day*?

I have not. Look at what our society requires to deal with the aftermath of alcohol-related issues.

We have Alcoholics Anonymous. We have rehabilitation facilities. Inpatient. Outpatient. We have lawyers who specialize in defending alcohol related crimes, drunk-driving in particular. We have lawyers who specialize in lawsuits related to alcohol related crimes, drunk-driving in particular. We have counselors. We have specialists. We have police units designed to deal with alcohol-related crimes. Alcohol plagues our society, but as we talked about earlier, our society accepts it, promotes it even, expects it often.

Quid De Me Ipso (What About Myself)

I need only examine my own life to know the truth. First, I wish I could get back the money that I spent on alcohol. Now, I wasn't an alcoholic; I was a social binge drinker. I drank with friends on the weekends and I drank to get drunk, that simple. I distinctly remember being fond of buying rounds of shots for my friends, Jagermeister was my favorite to start with, and I remember a round often running over $100. It was not uncommon to spend several hundred dollars a weekend or more on alcohol.

I look back at the things that I did while under the influence of alcohol and it makes me embarrassed and ashamed and I am so amazingly thankful that when God looks at me now, he sees the righteousness of Christ. Without Him, I would be a goner. But what about all of the people that I hurt while under the influence of alcohol. My wife and I had wicked, awful fights while under the influence of alcohol.

We still have issues on occasion, like any married couple, but we always engage with civility toward one another. We never seek to hurt each other and usually, we are honestly trying to overcome some type of miscommunication. Such was not the case when we were both fueled by alcohol. To be honest, much of it is hazy, but I remember the sick feeling in my stomach waking up the next morning after a horrible, alcohol-induced fight. I get a sickening feeling in my stomach to this day when I think of those days.

To be sure, I know great men of God that I respect greatly who consume alcohol. A friend of mine has been running an amazing ministry for many years and enjoys a beer with his son on occasion. Another Army buddy of mine, a great Christian man, will drink on occasion.

The best chaplain I ever knew, an anointed man of God if there ever was one, would drink on occasion. Sadly, I lost contact with this particular chaplain until just recently when I learned that the Army chaptered him out for what else, alcohol abuse and domestic violence. Somewhere along the way, alcohol took control and he began to abuse his wife. He quit the ministry altogether. He lost his entire family. Coincidence?

All of this has convinced me that alcohol is as much of a scourge on our society as any illegal drug. Alcohol is as much a tool of Satan as any drug. Alcohol has contributed directly and indirectly to the death and destruction of tens of thousands of Americans. I am sure that when the young man takes his first sip of a beer at a party, Satan smiles. I'm sure that when a young man gets home from war and heads straight for the bar, Satan smiles. I'm sure that when a couple fights and the man goes for the bottle, Satan smiles. I'm confident that when the man goes for his car keys because he's only had a couple, Satan positively beams, radiant. As my chaplain friend lifted drink after drink to his lips, I am confident that Satan giggled hysterically.

Alcohol, scary in its effects and even scarier in its prevalence, by itself would be a scourge of scourges. When combined with drugs, illegal and legal, alcohol provides the Devil with a truly effective and genocidal weapon. Of this I have become decidedly convinced. Decide for yourself.

Chapter 5 Discussion

REVIEW the Scripture passages cited in this chapter. In light of these:

1) Is drinking alcohol a sin? Does it matter?

2) How do you interpret the scriptural mandates concerning consumption of alcohol?

3) Why does this issue become divisive?

4) Would you attend a church where the clergy consumed alcohol? Why or why not?

5) Do you personally know someone who struggles with alcohol abuse or has made poor decisions while under the influence of alcohol?

6) Is the consumption of alcohol a Gospel issue or merely a point to agree to disagree upon?

Consider the following statement:

> Alcohol, scary in its effects and even scarier in its prevalence, by itself would be a scourge of scourges. When combined with drugs, illegal and legal, alcohol provides the Devil with a truly effective and genocidal weapon.

7) What are your thoughts on this statement?

8) Is this inflammatory speech/rhetoric or does reality vindicate this statement?

CHAPTER SIX

The Birth of Affliction

I can easily remember, very vividly, the saddest and most pitiful scene I've ever witnessed in my entire life. Just a few years ago I watched a woman hold her baby in court, crying desperately, sobbing, as she signed away her parental rights. She loved her baby but she could not overcome the demons of addiction that afflicted her. She didn't have the strength. Though she had made a few token attempts, she never came close to succeeding. The problem was, she liked the Scourge.

She liked the Scourge.

The little guy was born without a chance. His mother bore him into a morass of generational sin from which she could never escape. Her mother had always lived as a crack-addicted prostitute, so she became what else but a crack-addicted prostitute. This same cycle threatened to repeat itself with the little guy, easily, quite naturally. His lot was cast years before his birth, his conception, even. The natural flow of events would certainly have drawn him into the same patterned existence but for a miracle.

I've always wondered how many women who are addicted to a substance, tobacco even, abstain entirely during pregnancy. The little guy's mother didn't bother even keeping up pretenses of abstinence during hers. For the duration of her pregnancy, she smoked cigarettes. She drank. She smoked marijuana. She used crack or whatever else she could get her hands on or whatever else those who were willing to trade sex for drugs had on them. The evil system of affliction enslaved her. And for it, the little guy will bear a lifetime of consequences for her transgressions. Indeed, he has suffered greatly already, mentally, emotionally, physically. He just turned five years old.

The physical, mental, and emotional consequences of in-utero drug and alcohol abuse are well documented. The little guy typifies all of these. More than that though, through this tribulation, God has displayed his infinite power and unsearchable ways manifested in the unshakeable faith of a committed mother, my beautiful bride Ami.

Languishing in the northern Iraqi town of Mosul, near biblical Nineveh, in the winter of 2008, I received an email from Ami urging me to call home. Since I had arrived in late November, the weather had turned surprisingly cold especially for the desert with night time temperatures hovering below freezing. With my hands thrust deeply into my pockets, I made my way to the phone and computer tent to call home, more than a little worried.

“We’ve got a little guy,” Ami told me. I had left home merely two weeks ago and was certainly not expecting this.

I couldn’t believe it. The state had just completed our home study and approved Ami and I as foster parents literally the week prior to my departure. As they assured us, no one gets babies. Teenagers and sibling groups swell the foster system. Everyone fears teenagers and not many possess the commitment or resources to take in foster kids in large sibling groups.

The system does everything it can to keep sibling groups together. Often, brothers and sisters serve as the only source of stability in a foster kid’s life and sadly, many teenagers, most of whom languish in group homes, still seek foster parents and adoption even as late as 17 or 18 years of age. They still want a family it seems, even as legal adults.

But, we had a baby! Ami sent me a few pictures and I fell in love right away, immediately. I also knew, from the very first time I laid eyes on him, that he would be my son. Don't ask me how, but when I checked my email and saw this little brown guy looking solemnly back at me with dark and serious eyes across thousands of miles, continents, oceans, I just knew he would be my son one day. I cannot explain it.

Ami kept busy as always. My wife is, by nature, an exceedingly busy woman. She can hardly sit still normally, but when I deploy, she turns up the activity level a notch or two. Whether intentional or not, I believe it helps the time pass. Well, my middle daughter had a choir production that night and as they were walking into the school, Ami got the call from the Department of Children's Services. "We've got a healthy, Caucasian two-month old who needs immediate placement." It was December 9th, 2008. Ami told them that she was at a function but when they got home, to bring him on by.

That evening, DCS brought the little guy to our home. Packing boxes littered our home as Ami and the girls busily decorated for Christmas, but here was the little guy. Ami remembers that they had him wrapped up in a big blanket and all she could see were two little eyeballs looking out at her. Just like that, we had a new member of our family; we just didn't know for how long. Bubba arrived wearing a dirty onesie with a Walmart bag containing two diapers, a dirty bottle, two servings of formula, and oh yeah, he was brown.

We still laugh about this one. Ami immediately called her friend Heather had married a Hispanic man and asked her to come by. She and her husband have six children and she took one look at Bubba and confirmed, "That child ain't white!"

Bubba possesses the most beautiful skin you could imagine, a deep shade of tan year round and in the summer he turns immediately a deep, almost walnut color. All of my girls are immensely jealous of his skin tone.

However, for the first year of his life, his biological mother (more on her later) claimed that her boyfriend was the father. Now, to quote Forest Gump, "I ain't a smaht man", but Bubba's mother has skin paler than even mine as does her boyfriend. There was no way in the world this man fathered Bubba unless one or both of them possessed some seriously recessive genes. A DNA test later confirmed that the boyfriend had not, in fact, fathered the little guy.

That night, Ami ran to Walmart to get some diapers, formula and other baby stuff and Bubba fell asleep in my youngest daughter Haili's arms. Needless to say, she had already fallen in love with the little guy, as had the rest of my family.

Later, they gave Bubba his first diaper change. I'd give anything if I could've been a fly on the wall. Up to this point, my wife and I had only had our three girls. I can imagine the scene, my wife and three girls, ages 10 to 15, gathered around the little guy, nervously removing his diaper and giggling intently — always lots of giggles around my house even to this day — as they stared at male genitalia for the first time. My girls bless my home with a joyous hilarity and I can only imagine the giggles.

Initial Observations

ASIDE from the initial report from DCS on his race, they also reported that he was healthy. As it turns out, that aspect was similarly erroneous. For starters, Ami immediately noticed how skinny he was, borderline malnourished. She set about immediately to correct that but she also began to notice that this baby was just not a normal baby in some other very distinct but subtle ways. Aside from his skinny body, Bubba possessed no sleep schedule whatsoever, even one commensurate with a normal two month old. Ami chalked this up to his rearing to date along with the fact that he always required someone to hold him. If you set him down, even for a second, he would scream furiously, turning a deep shade of crimson in his fury. That wasn't all though, not nearly.

He hardly ate and when he was placed in bath water, he would wail an absolutely bloodcurdling scream, almost like a woman's scream, as Ami explained it. Additionally, his hands and feet almost always moved in a rhythmic kind of fashion, trancelike. Rarely did he lay still. There was definitely something unusual about the little guy, so Ami called DCS to ask why they placed him in custody.

As it turns out, at birth, Bubba had quantities of crack cocaine, methamphetamine, and marijuana in his system and so the state issued his mother, Nina, an order of protection. They restricted her from being alone with the little guy, so she went to live with her great grandmother, who agreed to supervise her child-rearing. Sometime later though, DCS learned that she was alone with the little guy, unsupervised, so they took him into custody and brought him to us.

Sometimes I stop and try to imagine what his life may have been like had his mother followed the rules and retained custody. I remember her telling me of an incident once that she found quite humorous. They had pit bulls where she lived and apparently at one point, two of them got into a fight in the kitchen over some meat. As they fought over the meat, blood began to spatter all around the kitchen including all over the little guy who lay nearby. Nina chuckled nervously as she relayed this story to me, clearly chagrined that her dogs would behave in such a manner. Again, I get moderately overcome when I think about the little guy growing up in that environment.

Anyway, Ami reported the abnormalities to DCS, but they had no record of anything so she actually went to the hospital where he was born — she used to work there — and secured his medical records. My determined wife was just getting started. His medical records, already a voluminous inch thick at two months of age, told a different tale, a tale of affliction. DCS's report of a healthy baby was anything but accurate.

Due to her crack use and fragile health, the doctors induced Nina into labor early; Bubba was born several weeks premature and for several weeks, he clung feebly to life. After birth, he developed a pulmonary edema causing his oxygen levels to bottom out. He required 100% oxygen for the first 72 hours of his fragile life. His blood pressure bottomed out as well requiring a saline bolus to keep it within range. His mother gave him an STD. She had developed three sexually transmitted diseases during her pregnancy and passed one of these on to Bubba. Thankfully, antibiotics did the trick. To this day, I thank God that she did not give him HIV or hepatitis.

Reading the reports, Ami's heart broke as she wept over what this little brown guy had lived through already. He could not have been born into worse conditions. Yet, we have seen and continue to see the miraculous in him. Severe and obvious physical abnormalities scar most crack babies. Bubba is not so obviously scarred. Unless you really knew what you were looking for, a cursory glance would only reveal a perfectly fine little guy. Such was not the case, though. Ami took him to see the pediatrician.

After a thorough examination, Dr. Aquino pulled Ami aside and asked inquisitively, "Do you know what you've gotten yourself into with this little one?"

Ami didn't know what she meant.

"He looks like a normal baby, but he's not a normal baby. No baby can be born into these conditions and be normal. And the older he gets, the more differences you will notice," she went on to explain. Bubba has proven her quite prophetic.

Thankfully, we live an hour from perhaps the best medical facility in the area, Vanderbilt University Hospital in Nashville. They have an amazing children's hospital and every type of unique specialist. Dr. Aquino referred Bubba to a pediatric neurologist and a pediatric urologist, since he wasn't circumcised and his foreskin had fused to the head of his penis due to a lack of cleaning.

They diagnosed him with asthma, fairly unusual for a newborn. Dr. Aquino prescribed him albuterol around the clock out of a nebulizer and Pulmicourt twice a day. I still remember how cute he looked with his little air mask on his face while taking his breathing treatments several times a day.

The urologist informed us that he definitely needed to be circumcised because of the condition of his foreskin and the neurologist wanted us to document all of his unusual behavior for six months in order to begin a profile of any conditions he may have. It didn't take long. It was just a few weeks later that he had his first seizure.

Fragility

I remember it vividly. One minute he was fine, running a fever but fine, and then all of a sudden, his eyes rolled in the back of his little head and his entire little body started jerking. Ami hollered that he was having a seizure. I immediately dialed 911 and ran into the kitchen where Ami held Bubba. That's when Ami screamed words that seared into my conscious for the rest of my life, "He stopped breathing!" Time stopped. My heart seized in my chest.

I can remember a handful of shear moments of terror in my life. This one took the cake. I remember very distinctly pleading instantly with God not to take him. I told the operator what was happening, handed the phone to my daughter Dairian, took Bubba from Ami, and prepared to administer CPR. Almost immediately, he started breathing again, on his own.

By this time, the ambulance was on its way. Ami met them in the road with Bubba in her arms. They put him in the back and the sight of him with an oxygen mask on, an IV in one arm, and three paramedics working on him almost brought me to my knees. I still get a lump in my throat up to this day thinking about it. At the hospital emergency room, they diagnosed him with febrile seizures, seizures due to a fever he was having. Needless to say, I probably could've used some medication myself.

For the next several months, we continued to monitor his progress. Very early, they diagnosed him with developmental delays. He wouldn't sit up, wouldn't roll over. He couldn't pick things up. At the age of 9 months, when many kids are starting to walk, my entire family, three daughters, Ami, myself, my mother, my father, gathered on the floor of our living room, cheering Bubba on as he tried and tried to roll over. Finally, he did it! We cheered as if we'd won the lottery. He was so determined.

He continued to move his hands and feet in an odd, rhythmic fashion and he had random fevers, several a week. Without warning, his temperature would rocket to over 100 degrees. Then he had another seizure. Helpless at work, I could only pray fiercely as Ami, with the help of our neighbor Mr. Roger, called 911 and waited for the ambulance again.

Back at the neurologists, they diagnosed him with epilepsy, seizure disorder, and prescribed Kepra, an anticonvulsant. He had barely lived a year.

His neurologist ordered an EEG of the brain, wanting to figure out from where the seizures were originating. The EEG was inconclusive for the source of the seizures, but it did show a large, unknown mass on one of his frontal lobes, quite possibly a tumor, not uncommon for crack babies. Ami and I grieved deeply, stricken with worry.

I believe in a God of miracles. The God of the Bible reigns Sovereign, Omnipotent, Merciful, and so we prayed. We prayed, hard. Ami went to visit a friend at her church. At one point, the pastor asked that if anyone had any prayer needs to come forward to the altar. Ami took the little guy and joined a couple of other folks who had come down to the altar. As the pastor came to her, he didn't ask any questions, but placed his hand on the little guys head and told my wife, "Your baby will grow up and live a long and fulfilling life." She had never even told him of her prayer need.

Tennessee Early Intervention got involved because of his developmental delays. They came to our home twice a week to work on him with his fine and gross motor skills. At one point, he had a severe allergic reaction to an unknown substance requiring another ER visit. His neurologist ordered an MRI of the brain to refine the results of the EEG. I still remember the little guy looking pitifully back over his shoulder at us as the nurses led him away to get the MRI. Poor little guy.

What the MRI showed was that he had several "spots" on his brain and a lesion on one of his lobes. A stroke in utero had almost certainly produced these abnormalities. What the MRI didn't show was the mass. Dumbfounded, the neurologist couldn't explain it. Did you catch that, there was NO mass. It was gone. Praise to the LORD! Though the MRI results showed some abnormalities, the stunned neurologist reassured us that everything looked okay and that the mass just wasn't there. We just needed to continue to monitor.

At some point, Bubba became our son. Nina, his mother, had struggled and tried, but she could not free herself from the demons of addiction. We took Bubba to see her regularly and it tore her up knowing that her sin, her failure, had afflicted her son as it had. We never made it a point to be too specific on his condition with her, but we didn't keep it a secret either. We felt like she should know. She loved him after all.

And so, she stood in court one fateful day, holding Bubba in her arms, sobbing softly as she signed her son over to us. It was, to date, probably the most pitiful scene I have ever witnessed. Here was affliction, the Scourge at its starkest reality, a mother giving away her child for the sake of the demons of addiction and in her heartache, I could almost guarantee that she got high that night. Such is the nature of this scourge.

Unusually Scourged

BUBBA thrived. He struggled, still struggles, but he thrived nonetheless. He continued to have seizures periodically, but gradually the doctors got them under control with medication. I must say that no matter how often it happens, I am never prepared emotionally or spiritually for a seizure. They are never routine. When it happens or when Ami tells me that he's had one, I can only think about that day in the kitchen and Ami screaming, "He stopped breathing!"

After the adoption, we took him back to the pediatric urologist for his circumcision. He informed us that the little guy's genitals were severely deformed on the inside. He had a urinary tract that was improperly routed and so in addition to his circumcision he required extensive reconstructive surgery. We've since discovered that this is a very common condition in crack babies. The very extensive surgery went amazingly well. We joke to this day that Bubba has a $10,000 hog!

Bubba has ticks, lots of them. As we have also learned, he has a combination of simple ticks, vocal ticks, and complex ticks. Simple ticks: he sniffs, he blinks his eyes … a lot, he rubs his nose, he grabs his shirt. Vocally, he does a really unusual thing and reverse stutters. Instead of the stuttering happening at the beginning of a word, it happens at the end. Very unusual. His complex ticks are combinations of movements. While moving, he will stop, touch his toes, touch his shins, touch his knees, and then stand up and continue moving. When having these ticks, he cannot keep from doing them. Lately he began to spit, often, every few seconds.

It is very cute, but very disconcerting as well. He rotates between them. He'll go a week or two without doing any and then he'll do one for a while or do them in combination. Every now and then he adds a new one. Recently he began doing this thing where he opens his mouth as wide as he can. He'll be talking right along and then, without warning, he'll just open real wide, and then continue talking as if nothing had happened.

Again, it's very cute, but the thought of him as a teenager, walking his prom date to the door, while stopping to touch his toes, shins, and knees unsettles me a bit. His neurologist explained that these may indicate Turret's syndrome or maybe even a future obsessive compulsive disorder diagnosis.

He has ADHD as well. I've never really given much thought to ADHD. At some point, school psychologists tried to diagnose my oldest daughter with ADHD. I believed she simply needed her rear end worn out. I've often believed that ADHD was used to justify poor behavior. I can say with absolute conviction, Bubba has ADHD.

Quite often, he simply cannot sit still. We home school and for that reason, decided against medication. We just deal with it as a part of how God made him. He would require extensive medication to make it in a public school and I'm just not ready to do that to him. We also resisted medicating him for his ticks for quite some time but recently have reluctantly allowed the neurologist to put him on a low dose of Tenex to try and suppress them a bit.

Our little guy has some other unique aspects to him as well. He burns hot and cold like no one I've ever seen. His emotions are raw and unfettered. When happy, he is joyous beyond belief. He has the sweetest giggle ever. When playing with his friends and when he and I are riding the wagon down the hill out front, he giggles with a hilarity that brings unimaginable joy to my life. I've yet to hear a greater sound in this world.

He has explosive anger. He doesn't just get mad, he gets furious. He rages. He explodes with volatility, trembling from within due to the sheer force of his anger. I've never seen rage in a kid like this before. When he gets his feelings hurt, even just a bit, he wails as if it were truly the end of the world. He has no middle ground.

At a pool party for someone's birthday once, he dropped his Popsicle on the ground. You would have thought someone was cutting his leg off or taking him from his mother. He screamed at the top of his lungs with a heartbroken rage. He wailed. He raged. He howled. We have learned over the years that there is very little recourse, just ride it out and maybe try to distract him with something else. Sometimes it works. Sometimes it doesn't. This time it didn't work and all of the kids were staring at him and he knew that all of the kids were staring at him and he screamed even louder at that, in his fury. When he finally calmed down, a nearby mother said to Ami, "Boy, he sure wanted that popsicle, didn't he?"

I don't know how Ami kept it together. She wanted to pull that mother aside and explain a few things to her, but to her credit she didn't. She just mumbled something and got Bubba a new Popsicle as his anger finally subsided.

Bubba never slept. I always say that I married a superhero and to prove it, I'll tell you that my wife went for about three years with no more than two hours of continuous sleep a night. Very early, it became apparent that it wasn't scheduling, Bubba just wasn't interested in sleeping. He would go to sleep okay, but never slept for more than a couple of hours in a row and when he woke up, he was up, and he wanted to be up, that was it. He did not want to lie in bed when he wasn't sleepy.

We tried everything. We tried bedtime routine adjustments. We tried herbal medications like Melatonin. Again, we resisted actual sleep medications which the doctors were more than ready to prescribe. The worst attempt was when we tried the Ferber technique. The Ferber technique says to just let the baby cry it out and eventually they will go back to sleep. They will learn to self-soothe. Well, Bubba was not having any of that. He refused to be Ferberized. Horrifically, he would scream at the top of his lungs for hours on end, hours. I've never seen such stamina.

Ami would be lying in bed with her hands over her ears, crying. It tore her up to hear him cry like that and not go to him. "Mommy!" he screamed, for hours. I finally discovered the only place in the house that you couldn't hear him. So each night I would take the cushions off the couch and make a pallet in the middle of the upstairs hallway, right outside the girls' rooms. Haili awoke to hearing me in the hallway. "Dad?", she asked hesitantly from her darkened bedroom, wondering what on earth I was doing. "Go back to sleep." Unfortunately, I am a very light sleeper. Finally, thankfully, we gave up on the Ferber method.

So for years, my trooper wife would get up, get him out of bed, and lay with him on the couch, all night, while he watched cartoons. As I would leave for work in the morning, sometimes they would just be going to sleep. As Ami laughs now, "Nights were when we bonded."

As you raise your children, you often wonder if they will ever understand the depths of a parent's love, to what extent you have gone for them. Almost decidedly, the answer is always a resounding, "no". Bubba will never even come close to comprehending the sacrifices that my amazing wife made for him and would willingly make again, without hesitation. She loves him that much. She loves him with a fierce and utter devotion that words can never explain.

I specifically remember one night, while my exhausted wife desperately tried to get some sleep, holding the little guy in my arms as he cried, begging him to go to sleep, begging God to make him go to sleep, crying myself. I wouldn't trade any of it for the world.

They finally did a sleep study on him and in a span of five hours he was aroused by his own brain activity over 80 times. The sheer pace of his brain activity woke him up repeatedly throughout the night. His brain moved as restlessly as his body. They offered sleeping pills again. We declined.

This lasted for four years or so, but over time it has thankfully diminished somewhat. He has good nights and he still has bad nights. As we have resisted medication, it seems as if he has started to develop the ability to go back to sleep on his own. He still wakes up several times a night, but not nearly like he did in those early years. Again, I have a superhero for wife.

Bubba has chronic constipation, always has. He has been on and off of varying types of laxatives for years and nothing seems to work. He will go days without using the bathroom. Finally, clutching his rock hard stomach, he'll end up sitting on the toilet, crying, holding Ami's hand, trying desperately not to poop because it hurts. It hurts badly. We still struggle to get this under control. The issue of toxicity concerns us and the doctors greatly.

He has meth mouth. As a defense mechanism, his little body channeled whatever nutrients it could get toward his vital organs to the neglect of things like his teeth. As such, all of his molars came in without enamel and his jawbones were extremely brittle and porous. We just recently took him for his second significant oral surgery. In total he had two teeth pulled, four root canals, four crowns installed, two root treatments, and bone treatments for his jawbone. Again, both surgeries went amazingly well. He now likes to show off his magic silver teeth, as he calls them, but at least he can chew solid food. The oral surgeon handed us his old teeth in a little case, and they are pathetic, tiny, rotten-looking, incomplete. They make me think of what might have been.

Triumph from Tragedy

THE demons of his biological mother's addiction, the Scourge, persecute Bubba to this very day. She used, he suffers, for life. As the one doctor told us, the older he gets, the more problems you will encounter and that has been the case, but we would not trade any of it for anything. It is just him. He is my little brown guy, he is my little Bubba, he is my little friend as I started calling him so many years ago. Miraculous, intelligent, talkative, energetic, affectionate, he has brought a joy to our family's life that I never thought was possible.

Thus, he will look solemnly at his mother and say, "I'm your special little guy, Mommy." God has wielded and continues to wield His power and grace through the unsearchable depths of a mother's love.

We could have a clearly deep discussion about the will of God and His purposes, His sovereignty, His providence, His work as it relates to the little guy. Why did God allow him to be afflicted by the sins of his biological mother? Why does God allow him to suffer, he was just a baby? Yet, when my little guy crawls into my lap and gives me squeeze and says in his husky little voice, "I love you Daddy", I know the answer to all of these questions, right then. Sometimes we ask the wrong questions.

God may still yet call Nina out of the darkness. As of this writing, she is out of jail, clean for a number of months, for the first time that she can remember. We still take Bubba to see her periodically. She just had surgery to repair a hole in her heart from years of drug use but unfortunately, she doesn't know any other way to live. The demons of addiction scourge everyone she knows, everything she knows, even her own mother. These demons work along family lines and I thank God that we could see the chain broken with the little guy. They are powerful chains indeed.

CHAPTER 6 DISCUSSION

THE book of James frequently addresses the actions of Christians in the world. Read James 2:14-26. In light of these passages:

1) Why do you think James felt led to write a book largely devoted to a Christian's actions?

2) In what ways do Christians today emulate verse 16 and figuratively say, "Go in peace, keep warm, and eat well"?

3) Why does James feel led to point out in verse 19 that, "The demons also believe — and they shudder"?

James 1:22 reads:

> But be doers of the word and not hearers only, deceiving yourselves.

4) What does James mean by this statement?

5) Have you ever deceived yourself in the way that James speaks of?

James 1:27 reads:

> Pure and undefiled religion before our God and Father is this: to look after orphans and widows in their distress and to keep oneself unstained by the world.

6) What is religion in the eyes of James? How does this apply today?

7) Why does James single out orphans and widows? Be sure to consider the 1st century context.

8) Who are the orphans and widows in 21st century America? Do Christians have any mandate or imperative to engage these issues based upon what James says?

CHAPTER SEVEN

Social Justice

I'VE considered aspects of social justice with respect to faith. What role does the church play in providing for social justice, caring for those who suffer, addressing societal ills? The impoverished, the downtrodden, have always sought a champion, an advocate.

After His temptation in the wilderness, the Bible tells us that Jesus returned to Galilee "in the power of the Spirit". (Luke 4:14) When he came to Nazareth, Scripture tells us that he entered the synagogue on the Sabbath as usual and that He stood up to read. It says that someone handed Him the scroll of the prophet Isaiah, and so Jesus read,

> The Spirit of the Lord is on Me,
> because He has anointed Me
> to preach good news to the poor.
> He has sent me
> to proclaim freedom to the captives
> and recovery of sight to the blind,
> to set free the oppressed,
> to proclaim the year of the Lord's favor.
>
> Luke 4:18-19

Some interesting events occurred after Jesus read these verses culminating with the people becoming enraged and literally attempting to throw Him off of a cliff, but let us focus on the actually reading. Consider who God has anointed Jesus to minister to as He quotes from the book of Isaiah: the poor, the captive, the blind, the oppressed. In other words, Jesus came to minister to those afflicted, the downtrodden, the suffering.

In the Beatitudes from His Sermon on the Mount, Jesus proclaims blessings for the poor in the spirit, those who mourn, the gentle, those who are persecuted for righteousness amongst others. Here again, Jesus turns His attention to the unlikely, not who many would expect, the undesirable. Countless times throughout Scripture, Jesus ministers to the unexpected and frequently, He ministers to them physically as well as spiritually.

Mark chapter 2 tells the story of the men in Capernaum who bring a paralyzed man to see Jesus but the great crowd prevents them from getting in to the home where Jesus stayed. Motivated and undeterred, they simply climb up to the roof, tear a hole in the ceiling, and lower the man down to Jesus. As soon as Jesus sees the man he says, "Son, your sins are forgiven." (v. 5) Some of the scribes nearby, speaking amongst themselves, actually begin to question the audacity of Jesus in thinking that He can forgive sins. After all, only God can forgive sins.

Jesus hears them and in response, heals the man. "Pick up your stretcher and go home," He simply says. Jesus heals the man physically. Jesus dealt with the physical and the spiritual time and time again. He forgives sin; He casts out demons. He heals people; He feeds people, thousands of people, miraculously. Jesus dealt with the physical aspect of suffering as often as He dealt with the spiritual or immaterial aspects of suffering.

On the extreme end of the spectrum from spiritual to physical, Liberation Theology demands corporate relief from physical suffering, societal and political freedom from oppression and affliction as a function of Christ's salvific work on the cross. Redemption, though personal, provides for a more corporate and collective salvation.

As the many find freedom in Christ, society cannot help but be changed for the common good. Many have even applied this slant to particular individual races, claiming the Gospel exclusively for the corporate freedom of a particular people group. Freedom becomes tangible, obvious, and overt. God subordinates the importance of personal redemption on behalf of the collective good. It exists, personal redemption, but corporate freedom trumps its importance.

Though I strongly dispute the premise that the Church exists primarily for this purpose and that any race or people group merits special consideration in this regards, it does contain an aspect of fundamental truth. The focus is just wrong. The Church, the universal church, should make things better. The local body of believers, the local church, should make things better on a local, community level. Herein resounds a simple yet profound truth that Jesus would not dispute. The Church should seek to improve societal conditions, to address the corporate suffering of the masses.

A Peculiar Dichotomy

I mentioned in chapter three that a peculiar dichotomy exists in our town and the more time I spend exploring our town, the more it strikes me. As I said, the second worst area of town, an area rife with affliction and oppression, lies but a couple of blocks from not only the biggest church in town, a several thousand member Baptist church with a campus the size of a small college, but at least five or six other huge churches of varying mainline denomination including Methodist, Church of Christ, Presbyterian, Episcopalian, and even a large Catholic church.

Our downtown area does not really have many tall buildings, but a survey from a distance reveals steeples. All you see are steeples, literally. Many reach hundreds of feet into the sky. In a perfect illustration of the point, it's only when you look down from the steeples that you can see the blight herein, the government housing, the poverty, the addiction. One could drive from this cluster of churches to the absolute worst area of town, an area even more rife with affliction, in just a matter of minutes.

Not only that, but if you drive through these two or three stricken areas, you'll notice, literally, a church on every corner. Now, these churches range in size from medium sized, well-maintained churches to smaller churches in strip malls or in odd, random buildings. Here, the denominations are not confined to the traditional. There are obviously a multitude of Baptist churches of every flavor … Southern, Independent, Free Will. There are Methodists, Catholics, Lutherans. There are a variety of what I assume to be Pentecostal or charismatic churches … the Apostolic Lighthouse, Church of New Jerusalem, Restoration House of Praise, even a Messianic Jewish congregation for good measure, right in the heart of the worst area in town.

As I drive around these areas and see the multitude of churches surrounded by urban blight I can't help but wonder, "How can this be?" How can the scourge of addiction exist so prevalently alongside a vast array of local bodies of believers and so close to rampant affluence? Are the churches active in addressing the issues of affliction? Are the affluent blind to the suffering so close at hand? When I think of the Light of Jesus Christ and the call to Christians to live as a beacon, a light unto the world, I wonder, how can so much darkness exist in and around this multitude of churches?

Provision

THE Bible clearly encourages social reform driven by the church. The Bible clearly encourages individual Christians to get involved and make a difference. Throughout the Old Testament,

God encourages His people to care for the poor.

God instituted the Year of Jubilee whereby every 50 years, all property would return to its original owners preventing any one person from acquiring the preponderance of wealth. (Lev. 25) God discourages indebtedness, equating indebtedness with servitude. In Exodus chapter 20, the Bible records God giving the Ten Commandments to the Israelites at Mount Sinai. In the following chapters, He gives them instructions in addition to the Commandments.

> You must not mistreat any widow or fatherless child. If you do mistreat them, they will not doubt cry to Me, and I will certainly hear their cry. My anger will burn, and I will kill you with the sword; then your wives will be widows and your children fatherless.
>
> If you lend money to My people — to the poor person among you, you must not be like a moneylender to him; you must not charge him interest.
>
> If you ever take your neighbor's cloak as collateral, return it to him before sunset. For it is his only covering; it is the clothing for his body. What will he sleep in? And if he cries out to Me, I will listen because I am compassionate.
>
> Exodus 22:21-27

Clearly God's desires to protect the vulnerable, widows, orphans, the poor, and He charges His people with this responsibility. His people are to serve as His hands and His feet carrying out His will. Call it social justice, but the Bible, and here specifically the Old Testament, offers irrefutable command after command to God's people to act, to do something.

Deuteronomy, the reiteration of God's law, amplifies some of these commandments to act. God tells his people again not to oppress the poor or downtrodden. Treat hired hands and foreigners with kindness and respect. Additionally:

> When you reap the harvest in your field, and you forget a sheaf in the field, do not go back to get it. It is to be left for the foreign resident, the fatherless, and the widow so that the LORD your God may bless you in all the work of your hands. When you knock down the fruit from your olive tree, you must not go over the branches again. What remains will be for the foreign resident, the fatherless, and the widow. When you gather the grapes of your vineyard, you must not glean what is left. What remains will be for the foreign resident, the fatherless, and the widow. Remember that you were a slave in the land of Egypt. Therefore I am commanding you to do this.
>
> Deuteronomy 24:19-22

God commands His people to leave their excess for the downtrodden and the helpless, the foreigners, widows and orphans. Lest they become haughty, He reminds His people, as downtrodden as the foreigner, the widow and the orphan are now, so too were you once, downtrodden as slaves in Egypt.

In the sovereignty of God, we see Ruth introduced to Boaz through this very practice, gleaning from the fields as Ruth, the widow, gleans wheat from the wealthy Boaz's fields. Their subsequent marriage yields a son, Obed, father of Jesse, father of David, in the lineage of Jesus Christ. The Bible, and here the story of Ruth, fully illustrates God's provision for the poor, the widow, and the orphan, His command for His people to act.

Countless other Old Testament texts prescribe action for God's people on behalf of the downtrodden. I've made the argument that poverty largely results from society collectively straying from Scripture, from God's plan, i.e. from sin.

Of course, the ultimate tale from the Old Testament of God's provision for the downtrodden resonates in the promised coming of the Messiah, fulfilled in Jesus Christ. The focus of Scripture speaks to the primacy of Christ as the Old Testament looks forward to His advent, life, atoning death and resurrection as the New Testament looks back to the same. Let us never lose this focus. Jesus Christ stands uniquely central to history and God's purposes for the redemption of mankind. Yet, in spite of this focus on the redemptive work of Christ, rather because of the redemptive work of Christ, God commands His people to make a difference, spiritually, physically, materially.

James and Works

WRITTEN by Jesus' half-brother, I have come to love the book of James as one of my favorite books in the Bible. Interestingly enough the church hesitated somewhat in adopting it into the Canon; it became one of the later books to be widely recognized as inspired. Problematically, it seems to focus upon good works, almost instead of or in place of faith. For this reason, some rejected the letter as non-inspired. Martin Luther, leader of the Reformation, author of the *Sola's* of faith even called it an "Epistle of Straw". The letter *seems* to stray from Paul's focus, indeed the Bible's focus, upon salvation and justification through faith in Jesus Christ alone, *Sola Fide* as it were, flummoxing many throughout the ages such as Luther. A quick perusal seemingly justifies this stance.

> You see that a man is justified by works and not by faith alone.
>
> James 2:24

You can quickly see how one could misconstrue James' intentions. Misunderstanding verses such as these has led to much of the consternation. Yet, an examination of the context proves fruitful. James didn't advocate salvation by or through works, but rather works as *evidence* of actual salvation, of faith.

> What good is it, my brothers, if someone says he has faith, but does not have works? Can his faith save

> him? If a brother or sister is without clothes and lacks daily food, and one of you says to them, "Go in peace, keep warm, and eat well," but you don't give them what the body needs, what good is it? In the same way faith, if it doesn't have works, is dead by itself. But someone will say, "You have faith, and I have works." Show me your faith without works, and I will show you faith from my works. You believe that God is one; you do well. The demons also believe — and they shudder ...
>
> ... For just as the body without the spirit is dead, so also faith without works is dead.
>
> James 2:14-19,26

James tells us that if you do not do good works, you accomplish nothing in spite any profession of faith you may have made. Do you actually have faith? Herein resides great power, power to change the world.

Unsurprisingly, Christian organizations comprise the most charitable organizations in the world. Arguably, one could make the same claim about the most charitable countries in the world. Anecdotally, after the earthquake in Haiti in 2010, no Muslim country contributed any relief, all of it coming from western, historically Christian nations.

Our faith should compel us to do good, to display the love of Jesus Christ in the flesh, the physical, to sacrifice and subordinate our own selves for the well-being of others, physically, materially. As a Christian, knowing that I have been saved from eternal damnation by Jesus Christ, out of sheer radiant exuberance I should seek to share Him with others.

A Christian should have perhaps no greater way to share the love of Jesus Christ than by meeting a need save for sharing the Gospel itself. Matthew 22 records Jesus responding to the Pharisees, an expert in the law who asks, I can't help but think with much sarcasm, "Teacher, which command in the law is the greatest?" Jesus, as always, leans upon the Word of God and quotes Deuteronomy and Leviticus.

> He said to him, "Love the Lord your God with all your heart, with all your soul, and with all your mind. This is the greatest command. The second is like it: Love your neighbor as yourself. All the Law and the Prophets depend on these two commands."
>
> Matthew 22:37-40

Jesus tells them to love God and love their neighbor, the greatest commandments. I would dispute the feasibility of man's capacity to do one and not the other. Clearly, from the context of Scripture and Jesus' own words, loving your neighbor is a natural result of loving God. Do you love your neighbor as yourself, your fellow man, or do you turn a blind eye to the plight of the downtrodden and the sinner, the lost and the lonely, the poor and the destitute?

Back to James, he tells us that faith that ignores others, faith that has no aspect of works, does not live. In fact, the absence of works connotes the absence of faith. This absolute truth should literally smack people coldly like a bucket of icy water.

Verse 27 of chapter 1 reads:

> Pure and undefiled religion before our God and Father is this: to look after orphans and widows in their distress and to keep oneself unstained by the world.

James describes true religion. Pure religion, undefiled religion. Religion has nothing to do with a church building or a worship service. Religion does not depend on preaching or listening to preaching. True religion takes care of orphans and windows. Simple. Keep yourself unstained by the world and care for orphans and widows. This simple concept represents religion, pure and undefiled.

You want to honor God, take care of orphans and widows. You want to obey God, take care of orphans and widows. Why orphans and widows though? There are people suffering all over the world, why orphans and widows? In first century Palestine, orphans and widows represented two of the most helpless classes of society, completely powerless and destitute, dependent entirely upon someone else for their very existence. Not coincidentally, orphans and widows will likely never be able to pay you back, to provide a return.

Back to chapter 2, James asks rather sarcastically, how can you tell someone to "Go in peace", to "be warm", to "be well" but not give them what it takes to have peace, to be warm, to be well? No Christian, indwelt by the Holy Spirit, could actually do this. The book of James speaks uncomfortably clearly on the issue. James condemns the tragic hypocrisy of those who claim Christ but ignore the reality of life on the street. James urges in chapter 1 verse 22,

> But be doers of the word and not hearers only, deceiving yourselves.

A Christian deceives himself by passing by the man on the street, looking the other way, and simultaneously professing Christ. James rails against the very notion. A Christian must *do* the Word, not just hear it. Let's generalize the concept. To walk by those who are afflicted, to ignore the downtrodden, the orphan, the widow, the addict, demonstrates that you actually do not possess faith. Christ does not reign in you. How could He? Jesus calls the Christian to action.

As he notes in chapter 4, verse 17,

> So, for the person who knows to do good and doesn't do it, it is a sin.

James speaks to the sin of omission as well as the sin of commission. In addition to doing things we ought not to do, we sin equally when we don't do things that we ought to do. God has given his people His commands when it comes to social justice, to caring for the poor, the sick, and the destitute and when we don't do what we know we should, what God commands throughout Scripture, we sin.

Jesus on Works

DURING His last week on earth, Jesus spent His time teaching in and around the Temple. At one point, as He was sitting on the Mount of Olives east of Jerusalem, his disciples come to Him in private and ask, "Tell us, when will these things happen? And what is the sign of Your coming and of the end of the age?" (Matthew 24:3)

Jesus proceeds to give them a great prophesy concerning impending persecution and the end of the age including His return. (Matthew 24) He then tells them the parable of the ten virgin and the parable of the talents before getting to a curious passage explaining the final judgment. Let's neglect eschatology for a bit and focus upon the facts of this judgment that Jesus speaks about in Matthew 25, commonly referred to as the Sheep and Goats judgment.

Jesus tells us that the Son of Man will come in glory with His angels and He will sit on the throne of His glory. (v. 31) All of the nations will be before Him and He will separate them like a shepherd separates the sheep and the goats, placing the sheep on His right and the goats on His left. To the sheep, those on His right, He will say, "Come, you who are blessed by My Father, inherit the kingdom prepared for you from the foundation of the world." (v. 34)

To those on His left, the goats, He will say to them, "Depart from Me, you who are cursed, into the fire prepared for the Devil and his angels!" (v. 41) He has blessed the sheep into His kingdom forever and cursed the goats forever. The criteria Jesus uses to separate the sheep and the goats should astonish us.

He says to the sheep in verses 35 and 36,

> For I was hungry
> and you gave Me something to eat;
> I was thirsty
> and you gave Me something to drink;
> I was a stranger and you took Me in;
> I was naked and you clothed Me:
> I was sick and you took care of Me:
> I was in prison and you visited Me.

They ask, Lord when did we ever see you in this condition? (v. 37-39) We never saw you like this. What do you mean? Jesus' response is telling, "Whatever you did for one of the least of these brothers of Mine, you did for Me." (v. 40) Jesus says that when they cared for the hungry, gave them something to eat, when they gave the thirsty something to drink, when they took in a stranger, when they clothed those without clothes, when they cared for the sick, when they visited the captives, they were in essence ministering directly to Jesus Himself. By serving as the hands and feet of Jesus, ministering to the least of these, meeting their physical needs, they are serving Jesus. Again, other than actually preaching the Gospel no greater way to serve God exists.

Contrast that with Jesus' judgment on the goats in verses 42 and 43,

> For I was hungry
> and you gave Me nothing to eat;
> I was thirsty
> and you gave Me nothing to drink;
> I was a stranger
> And you didn't take Me in;
> I was naked
> and you didn't clothe me,

sick and in prison
and you didn't take care of Me.

The goats object asking, Lord when did we see you in this condition? (v. 44) We never saw you like this. We don't know what you're talking about. Jesus responds "I assure you: Whatever you did not do for one of the least of these, you did not do for Me either." (v. 45) Jesus goes on, "And they will go away into eternal punishment." (v. 46) Jesus' words belie the serious nature of the issue. When one denies the hungry, denies the thirsty, deprives the poor, the destitute, the sick, one actually denies the Lord Jesus himself. This hermeneutical leap should drop everyone to knees of conviction and repentance.

When you turn a blind eye to the downtrodden, when you neglect the social responsibility of your faith, James would say that you have no faith. Jesus would condemn you to hell. Now, to be clear in our theology, taking care of the downtrodden, the poor, and the destitute does not save you.

Salvation comes through faith in Jesus Christ alone yet, taken in this context, Jesus tells us in Matthew 25 that these good works serve as an indicator of who He has saved, who has actually believed. You can recognize the sheep by the very fact that they act. They do these things, things that are physical, material.

Blinded to Affliction

I see the essence of this dichotomy fleshed out in our town, a condition that certainly exists elsewhere. I can envision the middle class family driving to church in their minivan. The mother fusses at the children as she tries to finish applying her makeup in the mirror. The teenagers are in disbelief that their parents actually woke them up this early on a Sunday of all days. The dad speeds along busily trying to make it on time, hoping church ends early enough to get to Cracker Barrel and then home for the football game. Maybe the pastor won't be his usual long-winded self this morning.

None of them notice the homeless man sitting behind the car wash or the hunched over addict limping down the sidewalk. None of them see the people languishing in the halfway houses down the side streets. None of them hesitate as they drive by the Department of Children's Services with immediate access to scores of orphans who have no family, no home. Not one of them realizes as they drive past the WIC office that this very facility represents the destruction of the family, the desperation of abandoned mothers, and the failure of a generation of irresponsible men. They cannot stop; they would almost certainly be late for church.

This is a Gospel issue; James would say it's a salvific issue. Jesus would almost certainly agree. I wonder how many who profess Christ actually have the dead faith to which James speaks. This disturbing thought truly keeps me awake at night.

CHAPTER 7 DISCUSSION

READ Isaiah 58:1-7. In light of this passage:

1) What is it that Isaiah denounces?

2) What in history demonstrated the need for God, through Isaiah to speak against this particular issue?

3) What is syncretism? How is it relevant to ancient Israel in Isaiah's time? How is it relevant today?

4) There is an apparent change of speaker in verse 3. Who is speaking in verse 3? What is God's answer?

5) Is there a way that modern Christians imitate verses 3b through 4?

6) What is the fast that Isaiah chooses in verses 6-7? What does he mean by this?

7) Apply these verses to the concept of social justice and a Christian's duty/obligation in the world. Has God called you to engage the culture? Has God called your local church to engage the culture? In what way?

This chapter deals with the concept of social justice and the Christian mandate to make a difference in society on behalf of Jesus.

8) Do you see the church making a difference in your community? How is it succeeding? Is it missing the mark in any way?

7) Do you see the similar issue of "a church on every corner" or is your particular city lacking churches? How does this apply to the application of social justice? Is this condition necessary for social justice?

CHAPTER EIGHT

Caveats

I fear I may cross a line with this chapter. No other account, with perhaps the exception of the little guy's, pains me more than this one for a variety of disparate reasons. This account is relevant, but it is personal and that's the struggle. It is my son. Questions pertaining to privacy and arrogance have plagued me and probably will continue to do so for some time. All that I've interviewed for this work fully endorsed me using their actual names and details. For those I didn't interview personally, including my son Dewayne, and for minors, I've changed names and details to protect their privacy while preserving the integrity of the account. Yet, in writing of my son, I've wondered, would he endorse this account?

My hesitancy exists in the potential for misunderstanding. I agonized over this chapter; I prayed over this chapter. I consulted my wife, my publisher and eventually came to the conclusion that this account is just too relevant to the overall body to exclude.

I pray that, as you read this account, you won't see condemnation or slander, but that you'll see three things. You'll see a tragic account of the power and danger of the Scourge. You'll simply see a father's love for his son. Finally, you'll see the awesome hand of God at work. As I struggled with this account, He showed up in a decisive way, seeing fit to deliver our son back home after many months of estrangement.

Driving Dewayne to jail the other day was quite surreal. He had materialized, literally, out of thin air, waiting on our proverbial and literal doorstep the night we got home from the beach. It had been nearly two years since he walked out the door in anger, seemingly never to return. Yet here we were, driving across town to drop off his son, my grandson, and then to the jail. We rode in silence for the most part, taking in the quiet Friday afternoon warmth, the late April sun on our faces. I wondered what he was thinking about, reflecting back over the years on how he had come to our family, the struggles and trials he had endured, the unsearchable sovereignty of God and His unknowable ways.

The Morning Rapper

I still remember the exact moment when I realized that we had a morning rapper living in our home. I was just getting ready to make some breakfast, eggs, at about five in the morning when I heard a sound.

Our home is incredibly quiet in the morning, the calm before the storm so to speak, just before the hustle and bustle of everyone getting ready for the day. Normally, I get up well before anyone else. As the first one awake, I absolutely cherish my quiet mornings. After reading the Bible for a bit, I'll sit quietly and pray, just me, God, and maybe some breakfast. The older I get, the more I come to cherish these times of silence and solitude.

Well, this particular morning, while frying some bacon, I heard something, or thought I did. I didn't pay it any attention and went back to cooking, but I heard it again. It was a … beat, or something. *What the heck was that?* I left my bacon to fry and stepped quietly into the hallway. I heard it again. *It was a beat! What was that?*

I quietly crept down the hall toward the bedroom doors, avoiding the squeaky board at the top of the stairs, and came adjacent to the Big Man's room. Sure enough, I'd heard a beat. I put my ear to the door and I heard … rapping! He was rapping in there! Five o'clock in the morning and he was in there, ironing his shirt to get ready for school … and rapping! I stepped back, thought to myself with a smile, "We have a morning rapper!" and went back to my breakfast.

I know no one battling the demons of addiction more than Dewayne. I sometimes wonder about his awareness of their existence, these demons. To be sure, his personal addiction is in its infancy, weed only to this point. To the best of my knowledge, he has yet to try any hard stuff. Ami and I have recently come to the conclusion that Dewayne self-medicated with marijuana, treating scourge with the Scourge, if you will.

Ami, the more attentive of us, became the first to realize his once burgeoning usage. My wife notices everything — I almost feel sorry for our kids as they can never get away with anything. One particular night, she gets a feeling so she gets up and goes to the front door to look out. There, in the dead of the night sits a car, idling quietly, one of Dewayne's friends. Slowly, obviously, the car backs to in front of the vacant lot down the street; the attempt at being unobtrusive was fairly comical. From our front porch, Ami sees four red-hot embers flare and smoke immediately emanate from the windows.

Well, my wife did what any mother would do and fired off an angry text to Dewayne telling him that she knew what he was doing and that if he didn't get in the house that second, she was coming down there! Instantly, the doors of the car flung open and four teenage boys scattered in different directions, heads down. Dewayne and D-Win came guiltily slinking in the front door while Ami stood there angrily with her arms crossed.

Over these last few years, God has shaped me into more of a realist than I ever imagined I'd become. As such, I've reached the conclusion that almost all teenagers will try marijuana at some and I'm quite confident that statistics will bear this fact out. This does not mean that I consider it acceptable or not dangerous; reality forces consideration if not actual accommodation. With Dewayne, Ami and I hoped that this was merely experimentation, an aberration. We discovered soon enough that the reality was quite different than we had hoped for.

The first time Dewayne left our home, he literally kind of just hung around. He slept at various friends' apartments, his girlfriend's home, anywhere anyone would let him crash and eventually, when he wore out his welcome everywhere else. He even slept in the woods across the street from our home. Ami would take him PB&J sandwiches and stash them in his bag that he kept in the woods.

He just hung around, smoking weed. He even took the tarp from the garage and built a little lean-to behind my oldest daughter's apartment. Eventually, she complained to me that he repeatedly broke into her apartment and drank all of her milk. He did what he had to do. He always has.

Yet, we were only just beginning to peek behind the veil. At this time, I could not have imagined the extent of the scourge in Dewayne's still young life. Yet this thread of his existence precedes his very conception, running back to before he was even born. The demons of addiction torment Dewayne secondhand, by proxy. He inherited this scourge.

> But He will not leave the guilty unpunished, bringing the consequences of the fathers' wrongdoing on the children and grandchildren to the third and fourth generation.
>
> Exodus 34:7b

I believe in generational sin. After all of these years, after all of this time, I believe it with all of my heart. The closer I've come to know those who battle the Scourge and those around them, the more I see generational sin run its course. Not that generational sin is confined to addiction, but generational sin is a fact. Drug abuse runs in the family. Alcoholism runs in the family. Domestic violence runs in the family. No researcher will deny these facts. Normally chalked up to genetics or to socialization during upbringing, generational sin as spoken of in the Bible afflicts countless many but I don't need a sociologist to point these realities out to me. I've witnessed it personally.

When looking at the Bubba's life and now Dewayne's, it became *obvious* that sin runs along family lines, that sin runs in the family. One would have a very difficult time denying this simple fact. Yet, this invites some fairly profound theological questions. Is God punishing Dewayne for the sins of his father, the sins of his mother? Possibly. I do not claim to understand the mind of God.

The sins of Dewayne's father and mother have scourged Dewayne's existence from his very birth, an absolutely undeniable conclusion. The consequences for their choices have run deep, for generations. He exists in the crucible, a second generation. Sadly, the Scourge busily afflicts a third. Barring the miraculous, which I definitely do not, I can already see the seemingly inevitable continuation of the cycle. The Scourge runs that deep. Nothing can satiate or appease it.

It's Not Your Fault

FREQUENTLY, as I tuck one of our other little guys into bed, a three year old in the clutches of the Scourge, I'll whisper to him over and over, "it's not your fault." He'll look up at me with his solemn brown eyes and say, "okay, Papa" actually seeming to understand. I desperately want him to know.

Dewayne came to us as the caricature of the system kid. All of the bad things about the system — and the system certainly has its flaws — manifested themselves in this quiet young boy, a young man who fell through the cracks, literally. A sweet, shy, and quiet young man, the first time we met, he wouldn't even look up at anyone; he just sat there awkwardly staring down at the table. Ami and I had prayed about Dewayne for years.

Once we decided to become foster parents several years earlier, we immediately started praying to God to send who He would. Several organizations have websites that post profiles of kids who are available for adoption and one of the very first profiles we looked at was Dewayne's. About 13 or 14 years old, He spoke about wanting a family with brothers with whom he could play basketball.

Obviously uncomfortable on film, he spoke so softly you could barely hear him. Intermixed with clips of him speaking, the video showed him riding his bike around a run-down looking neighborhood, but his eyes. His eyes pierced, resonating with a sadness, a certain vulnerability.

One look and I knew that he had taken the brunt of what the world had to offer. I knew that my gaze had fallen upon the Scourge. Our entire family fell in love immediately and all of my girls instantly exclaimed, "We want him!" So we began making phone calls.

I must say that from day one, our inquiries into Dewayne did not go well. We finished our home study and sent it in for review but could not get anyone to look at it or even show it to Dewayne. His caseworker wouldn't take any action. His caseworker's boss wouldn't take any action. We were given the runaround for months on end. The months became a year and finally, after having made absolutely no progress, we gave up. We didn't understand.

I thought that they would by dying to get him out of the system. Dewayne was available for immediate adoption and we were offering our family up to adopt him. Yet, for whatever reason - I have my speculations - we could not generate any traction. We concluded that God did not want this to happen; this was not His plan. *Why would God not want an orphan to be adopted?*

About a year later, Ami and I attended a foster parent

conference in Nashville. Various foster agencies, adoption groups, and private organizations filled the convention center with booths and displays. You could sign up for various classes, inquire about services offered, ask questions. It was all very similar to any other professional conference, this one just centered upon foster children and adoption.

As Ami and I browsed the various booths and displays, idly chatting, something caught her eye. The displays typically included many colorful pictures of different children in the system — it is much more difficult to deny an orphan once you put a name to a face. As I turned my head to see what she was looking at, Ami made a beeline for the lady behind the booth. It was Dewayne!

Ami asked the lady at the booth about him and she told us that he was available for immediate adoption, had been for some time. Amazed and livid at the same time, amazed that God had thrust him back into our lives, but livid that Dewayne languished in the foster system unnecessarily for over a year, Ami and I went back to work.

Ami sent emails, she made phone calls with a vengeance and remarkably, we still could not get any traction. Finally, I emailed the president of the Tennessee Department of Children's Services outlining the issue and made some fairly damning claims and accusations. I even played the race card. It worked! We had a meeting set up with Dewayne within a week. Sixteen years old by this time, Dewayne was currently living in a group home in Jackson, Tennessee.

He had toiled in the system for much of his life, since he was about five. The *System*, sadly necessary, frequently swallows kids whole and then spits them out the other end, eighteen and angry. As advertised, the kid enters the system under the care of a loving foster family as the foster parents support the birth parents in rectifying whatever situation required the placement in the first place. The cooperative function culminates in the return of the children to the birth parents.

Were in not for the nature of the Scourge, this may actually occur with more regularity. Instead, Dewayne's case resonates with sadly, stereotypical circumstances.

He never knew his father who purportedly lived in Chicago. Later, he would learn that the man he had thought was his father was not, yet more uncertainty in an already uncertain life. His mother was, you guessed it, an addict. The details of his background are sketchy, hazy, as among other things Dewayne does not and often will not communicate very well.

I do know that he witnessed violence. He witnessed a murder. He witnessed his mother do drugs, repeatedly. He witnessed violence against his mother. He saw other people do drugs. He witness, he lived, all of the seedy, unspeakable, and despicable aspects of the scourge of addiction and all that comes along with it: violence, sexual sin, despair, turmoil. Dewayne grew up in the classic inner-city, drug-laced ghetto.

He actually toured us through Frayser at one point. We had to go back to Memphis for a court hearing on his behalf and while there, he asked to show us his neighborhood. A onetime industrial area to the north of Memphis, Frayser epitomizes urban decay. The factories closed down decades ago leaving behind nothing but industrial pollution and poverty.[1] Run down houses with boarded up windows line the remarkably vacant streets. It looked exactly like I thought it would and it broke my heart. We even recognized the street that Dewayne rode his bike down in his profile video.

Because of the blight of addiction, Dewayne was torn from the one constant in his life, his birth mother. Yet, he holds his mother, to this day, in an amazingly high regard, on a pedestal. He worships her despite knowing that her addiction put him into the system in the first place. Before she died last year, he used to fantasize about becoming a famous rapper and rescuing her from life, from her affliction.

Most system kids feel similarly about their birth parents. No matter how badly their parents have mistreated them, they still hold their parents in a high regard. They cling to their parents or rather, to the very idea of their parents. The system rightly seeks reunion of the children with the birth parents. Therefore, potential foster parents learn very early that no matter how horribly the birth parents have behaved or treated the kids, they must never disparage them. Dewayne was torn from the only thing he knew, his mother. There was definitely an incident of some kind; we just never learned what it was.

From there, the system swallowed Dewayne whole and bounced him from home to home in what was to become a cycle. As a withdrawn and shy young boy, Dewayne would, and still does, avoid confrontation at all cost and when he does not like the way things are going, he leaves. He's a runner, always has been. When the situation gets tight, he leaves, without hesitation. He would show up to a foster home, feel mistreated at some point, and leave, at which point the foster family would give him back to the system.

Repeatedly, Dewayne would run and get caught, requiring DCS to find him a new home. Over and over it was reinforced to him that no one would love him unconditionally, no one would love him through the things that he did. If he misbehaved he was gone. Finally, he ended up in the group home in Jackson two hours up I-40 from Memphis. He ran again and this time, the police found him many miles down the interstate, walking back to Memphis, back to his mother, back to the demons that had put him in the system in the first place. In my mind I can actually very clearly see him walking down I-40 toward Memphis.

At Last

WE finally met Dewayne in an extremely awkward conference at the group home in Jackson. Ami and I along with my three nervous daughters sat around a long table anxiously waiting for a number of minutes before he showed up with the case worker.

I can only imagine how he must have felt. I honestly feel like we may have actually been the first white people he had ever seen. *What did they say to him? What did he think?* Here was this family of white folks that wanted to adopt him. We had never met him. *Why would we want to do that?*

It must have seemed very strange to him and so we sat around the table and the social workers tried to get him to talk and he just mumbled quietly and looked down at the table. It felt like a very awkward hour or two and I'm sure it felt like an eternity to him, but eventually we left. Amazingly though, we received word a few days later that he liked us. He wanted to come and visit and maybe be adopted! God had answered our prayers at last, after all of this time.

It took some final haranguing, but DCS finally sent Dewayne for a weekend visit which went great and then we received the word we had waited for. He wanted to be in our family, he wanted us to adopt him. What had taken over two years at this point, now only took another month.

Within four weeks of meeting him for the first time, we went back to pick him up for good. Without hesitation, he climbed right inside of our ugly 15 passenger van and jumped to the front between Ami and me to talk on the way back. We even stopped at Taco Bell to celebrate the opening chapter of our newly complete family. Everything felt right, complete. We just knew that Dewayne would relish his chance to be free of the system and free of the life that had hung him out to dry, free of the demons that plagued him. Yet, the demons would not be so easily deterred.

Things went great initially, call it a honeymoon, but it soon became apparent that Dewayne had some unique issues from his years as a system kid. For starters, we weren't really sure what grade to put him in and neither was the school system. He was getting ready to turn 17 and apparently had just enough credits to almost be in the 9th grade. Obviously they couldn't put him in the 9th grade at 17 so they developed what they refer to as an

Individual Education Plan (IEP).

Basically, Dewayne had no hope of catching up to his peers so they have a system whereby a kid who lags behind and has an IEP can take a series of Gateway tests. If they pass the tests, similar to exams, they are awarded a diploma. It's that simple and the rewarded diploma appears indistinguishable from the diploma earned by kids who do all four years. And they train them to the tests. To me, it reeked of, "Let's just get this kid out of the school system." He had obviously just been pushed along all of these years and as much as it grieved me, we didn't know what else to do and neither did the school.

Dewayne had some other peculiarities as well. It soon became apparent that the most basic things that you and I might take for granted just did not exist. He had no concept of time and literally did not consider anything further out than about the next five minutes. The thought of getting him to think about the future and teaching him how to set short-term and long-term goals still brings a smile to my face. We had many conversations in my truck that went like this:

> Dad, "So, Dewayne, you're almost 18, what about the military?"
>
> Dewayne, "No, that sucks."
>
> Dad, "What about college?"
>
> Dewayne, "Yep, I want to go to college."
>
> Dad, "What do you think you might be interested in studying?"
>
> Dewayne, "I don't know. Sumthin'."
>
> Dad, "What about business?"
>
> Dewayne, "No, that sucks."
>
> Dad, "Well what do you think you'd like to do? The sky's the limit."
>
> Dewayne, "I like to draw, maybe play basketball."

And on we would go. We finally hit the jackpot at one point though when I mentioned being a barber. Dewayne sat up instantly and said, "Yes, I want to do that."

He clung to this one thing, the notion of being a barber. He cut his own hair and anyone else's that would let him and did a great job and so he wanted to go to barber school. His excitement was palpable.

Additionally, Dewayne shared another common trait with many system kids and many who are scourged by addiction, that they see people as a resource. Ms. Laurel actually pointed this out to us as we were discussing one of the Covenant House kids with her. She pointed out that this particular kid was exhibiting classic addictive behavior, seeing people as a resource, a means to an end. Dewayne was a survivor, had adapted to his conditions, been required to fend for himself. He exhibited very little loyalty to people. They had never been loyal to him, so why should he be loyal in return.

No one had ever taught him the most basic and simple tasks in life. He didn't know how to drive, which we worked on. He didn't know how to work. No one had ever taught him the value of a hard day's labor. No one had ever taught him about how to earn money. No one ever taught him about integrity and values and here, the struggle became that much more challenging, the conflict that much more intense.

It soon became obvious that he possessed not just a slightly different set of beliefs, but a completely and utterly different and distinct set of values, morals and ethics. Our family's life and morals revolve primarily around our Christian faith and to the best of our ability, we stick to the teachings of Jesus Christ in the day-to-day conduct of our lives, but Dewayne had existed in survival mode for many years now and no one had taught him these things.

I still smile when I remember an early conversation he had with Ami. The ladies love Dewayne. They've always loved him and he knows how to talk to them. One of the first nights he disappeared, I happened to find him sitting outside a gas station on Langston drive with a cute little gal sitting in his lap and a big, guilty smile on his face.

As a Christian family, we do not approve of nor condone nor enable premarital sex. Females are not allowed in boy's bedrooms and vice versa. Again though, we're realists. Ami and I figure that if they are going to do it they will. We just don't want to make it any easier for them.

Dewayne could not and does not and has never understood this and in one of our early conversations about it, he accused Ami of being an inhibitor to his affairs — not the actual phrasing he used. It absolutely miffed him that we would try to inhibit his sexual exploits. It perplexed him. He didn't understand at all. I remember well the look of sheer puzzlement on his face as we discussed the rightness of sexual purity.

So, here was a young man amazingly ill-equipped to live life. He had no life skills, no knowledge that he did not have life skills, no moral compass to guide him, and no idea of where he was going or what he wanted to do. The things that a Dad and Mom were supposed to teach him, particularly a Dad, just weren't there. No one had taught him what it meant to be a man; his notions and concepts of manhood he literally derived from various rap artists, Lil' Boosie being a favorite.

In one of the last conversations Dewayne and I had, I called him out for continuing to pursue other women with no consideration for his pregnant girlfriend. As he explained to me in exasperation, "This is what a man does!" He was clearly as frustrated as we were.

Running

I loathe the victim mentality, but the system, the addictions of his mother, the scourge of his parents afflicted Dewayne in unsearchable ways. I can't begin to imagine the effect that abandonment alone must have had. Many folks are afflicted greatly *just* by abandonment. Dewayne endured that and more, unspeakable affliction. I cannot fathom the effect this has had on his psyche.

So he ran, often. He ran and we would worry and then welcome him home after a day or two and then talk it out and things would be good for a while and then he would run again. The cycle would repeat. At first, we were heartbroken every time he ran. *What were we doing wrong? What could we do differently?* After a number of times though, everyone in the house became somewhat numb to it. Eventually people even began to get annoyed at how he would run off when things didn't go his way.

Dewayne turned 18 and began to want what all 18 year olds want, freedom and independence. We wanted that for him. The only problem was his complete unpreparedness to manage freedom and independence. I guess that no one is ever really prepared, but this was a little different.

His one attempt at holding down a job at Sonic did not go very well. Dewayne never operated well under stress. He would simply fold and go vegetative under pressure, literally, not a helpful quality in the fast food business, a fairly high-stress environment.

Probably due to that, he had a boss that did not treat him very nice and after a day or two on the job, he just stopped going. We would drop him off at work and unbeknownst to us, he would just leave. For several weeks, we lived under the assumption that he was going to work until driving away one day, I happened to look into my rearview mirror and see him run across the street away from Sonic.

So his one job ended in unsuccessfully. He had no money, no job, no life skills, but wanted desperately what every 18 year old young man wants. He began to resent any attempts we made to have him follow house rules, like don't stay overnight at girl's houses, etc. He could not understand why he couldn't just do what he wanted. And then he met Jasmine.

In short, he met a girl, got her pregnant and left. No brief synopsis could ever capture the next four or five months of pain and anguish and turmoil, tearful pleadings on our behalf for him to talk with us, him walking out angrily over and over, him getting arrested once, twice.

Since he wouldn't stop smoking marijuana in our house and in our neighbor's yard, I finally asked him to leave. He moved in with his girlfriend and a number of months later, after the birth of his son, they all moved to Memphis. Memphis drew him back; he couldn't stay away. Shortly after moving there, he abandoned his girlfriend and son and disappeared into his affliction. Jasmine and their son eventually moved back home.

Almost a year later and homeless, Dewayne walked into a crisis center in Memphis and called home. We assured him that we loved him and missed him. He left the center the very next day. After speaking with his aunt, we learned that he had been bouncing around Memphis for some time, staying with whoever would put him up. From the crisis center, he stayed with his aunt for a number of days but no one wanted the Scourge in their home and since Dewayne wouldn't walk away from it, everyone ended up asking him to move along. His aunt did not specify what he was into, only assured us that it was "nothing good".

Again, I do not believe in victimization. We've tried to teach Dewayne, in all of this, to take responsibility for his actions, something we teach all of our kids. Dewayne was shaped; he was shaped by his upbringing. *What would I be like had I grown up under similar circumstances?*

I had a great home with two loving parents. I had a father who taught me things like what it meant to be a man, how to work hard, how to live life. He taught me values and ethics, not that my upbringing was perfect, whose is, but it definitely shaped me into the man I became and I still screwed a lot of things up. *What kind of man would I have become without a father to teach me these things?*

To be sure, plenty of men grow up and thrive despite these kinds of circumstances. Dewayne may still become one of them. We are far from giving up hope.

Yet, I look at what addiction has wrought in his life and it saddens me. His aunt also confided in Ami and me that Dewayne's mother, her sister, used frequently during her pregnancy. Once we learned this and the types of things that prenatal substance abuse does to a baby, the pieces fell into place. Addiction robbed my son of a childhood. Addiction robbed my son of a mother and a father. Addiction robbed my son of love and affection. Addiction robbed my son of a chance, it would seem. Like many system kids, he became a survivor, a taker, a user.

His mother's addictions scourged Dewayne severely. I don't know if his father was an addict, he just wasn't present. The Scourge runs rampant; I see countless young men and women who are equally as afflicted. The blight of addiction and its effects afflicts all segments of our society, penetrating generations and generations to come in a self-perpetuating, and ever worsening, cycle of despair. It tears families to shreds, often before they even begin, as with Dewayne's.

A New Scourge

UNFORTUNATELY, with Dewayne, I can already see another generation of affliction developing. I believe in miracles. I worship a good and mighty God who reigns sovereign and holy and powerful. Barring His intervention, my grandson, Dewayne's son, already suffers for the sins of his grandparents, Dewayne's parents. As a scared, 20 year old young man, Dewayne possesses only a vague notion of what fatherhood means, of what manhood means. I still remember what an incredible idiot I have been on many occasions as a father and I am on kid number five. *What would I have done as* *an ill-equipped father at 20?*

I pray that Dewayne would become the father his son so desperately needs. Dewayne and Jasmine's relationship did not survive the move to Memphis as Jasmine herself comes from an equally broken background with, unsurprisingly, prenatal substance abuse by her mother; virtually every young lady in her family with a child has no relationship with the birth father. As such, the odds are clearly stacked against my grandson.

God designed the family in the best way, a man and a woman, together as husband and wife, raising their children. This is the best way. This is God's way. Kids raised by single parents struggle in almost every facet of life. It is a fact and it is an epidemic.

Brookings Institution calculations of census data for 2009, a recession year, show that adults who do three things, graduate from high school, have a job, and are at least 21 before marrying and having children, have a 70% chance of making the middle class and about a 2% chance of living in poverty. For people who did not meet any of these factors, it is nearly reversed, a 77% chance of living in poverty and a 4% chance of making middle class or higher.[2]

Young women who have a high school degree or less, increasingly do not marry and roughly 40% of their babies are born outside of marriage which quadruples the chance that they and their children will live in poverty. Children raised in single-parent homes have more developmental problems and lower academic achievement than those raised by married parents, effectively perpetuating the cycle of poverty and destitution. Anecdotally, almost every prisoner in Western Kentucky State Prison was raised by a single parent.

Dewayne's son, my grandson, already languishes in a life that was given to him. He inherited the Scourge from his father, from his mother. The affliction wreaks havoc on subsequent generations. The Scourge runs deep and destroys along family lines. I have come to learn that only the miraculous can break these chains, these lines of generational destruction.

The Grand Weaver

YET, I testify that God does the miraculous. Ami and I prayed fervently for *years*. We prayed for Dewayne's safety, that God would protect him on the streets. We prayed for his salvation. We prayed for his son, that the Scourge would not afflict him. We prayed that Dewayne will become the man that his son so desperately needs him to be. God answers prayers.

While typing this last part, Dewayne peacefully sleeps in his old bedroom with his young son beside him. You see the Author continually crafts, continually spinning the yarn of our very existence. In our finiteness, we are privy to but a glimpse, a snapshot of the reality of the present and a continually blurring memory of days long past. Yet there exists an infinite drama yet to unfold and He busily crafts events, shaping reality, forging life all in accordance with the good graces of His predetermined plan.

Such as it is with Dewayne. We hadn't heard from him other than some sporadic social media communications in quite some time when he called, out of the blue. Ami and I both waited expectantly and it happened, he showed up as if on cue.

After a couple of awkward hugs he came inside to hang out while we unpacked from our trip to the beach. Ami and I exchanged nervous looks. *Why was he here? What did he want? Was he clean?* Over the years, Ami and I have developed a rule that we never violate. So, she ran to Walgreen's for an over-the-counter drug test. I informed him that I loved him but that if he had anything in his system, he couldn't stay until he was clean. He said he understood and reassured us very calmly that he was clean.

So there I sat, in my garage on the weight bench, holding my breath as I waited for six little red lines to appear on the test indicating the absence of illegal drugs. After a few minutes,

Dewayne shyly poked his head in the garage door followed closely by Ami. I looked down at the test. Slowly, maddeningly, the lines appeared, one by one, all six. He was clean. I almost cried in relief as I looked at Ami and mouthed the words, "He's clean". She teared up instantly, embraced Dewayne, and told him how proud she was, welcoming him home.

We spoke for quite some time, right there in the garage, and I asked him what he wanted to do. He told us he wanted to make things right. Could he see his son and would I take him to jail to turn himself in for pending charges? We assured him that we would help him do both and that we were incredibly proud to have him as a son.

And just like that, the threads of our lives intersected once again as the Grand Weaver spins his wheel. I don't claim to know what the future holds but hope springs eternal. Dewayne has a court date next week and his son spent the week with us. Walking into our church for Easter Sunday, I was so proud to see all of our friends who know Dewayne welcome him back, loving on him, hugging on him and generally making a fuss over his very presence. He humbly ate it up. Though as quiet as ever, I could tell he was beaming inside.

My spirit soars with the hope of the unknown. For so long, we've seen only the devastation of the Scourge ripping apart a young man's life before it really even had a chance to begin. Now it appears that at least for the moment, the demons have been beaten back, restrained. Perhaps the Scourge has run its course in this family.

CHAPTER 8 DISCUSSION

READ God's statement to Moses in Exodus 34:6-8.

1) How do you reconcile the description of God in verse 6, "compassionate and gracious, slow to anger and rich in faithful love and truth" with verse 7 whereby the consequences of the father are visited upon the children and grandchildren?

2) Is this fair? Why would God allow or even ordain the consequences for a father's actions to afflict his children and grandchildren? Are there other accounts in the Bible that are difficult to reconcile with a loving God?

3) Can you see the notion of generational sin manifest in your community today? Your family?

4) How does Moses respond to God's statement in verse 8? Why would he respond in this fashion?

5) Some would argue that this is an example of God being unloving and cruel. How would you respond to that statement?

This chapter speaks to the affliction of broken families amongst other topics:

6) Do you believe the biblical mandate that marriage is between a man and a woman? Why or why not? Does it matter?

7) Have you seen the impacts personally of a broken family, divorce, birth out of wedlock?

8) What is the only hope for those afflicted by the sins of their fathers? How would you communicate that to someone similarly afflicted?

CHAPTER NINE

Cannae

THE morning of August 2nd, 216 B.C. broke clear and crisp. A light breeze and the rising sun accompanied the young Roman infantrymen as they approached the awaiting Carthaginians on the plains of Cannae. With the Aufidus River to their right and numbering nearly 90,000 including the cavalry on their flanks, the Romans led by Varro were an eager bunch, hungry to engage and defeat Hannibal.

His invasion of the Iberian Peninsula had been wildly successful thus far and the Carthaginians' confidence grew with each victory. Just months prior, Hannibal seized the sizeable supply depot at Cannae and with each tactical victory, the threat to Rome itself became that much more palpable.

Across the battlefield, a young Gallic (French) infantryman stood in formation awaiting his death. Wearing no armor and carrying but a long sword, he stood shoulder to shoulder with the other conscripts in Hannibal's army as the Roman legions advanced. Hannibal's tactical prowess had carried the day previously but here, outnumbered at least 2 to 1, defeat seemed certain.

The sound of 150,000 men and countless horses maneuvering on the battlefield, with the cries of battle, shouted commands of the officers, and the blowing dust must have rendered the scene incredibly confusing.

Confident, Varro arrayed his forces in a deeper than normal formation and pressed directly into the center of Hannibal's lines seeking a quick penetration and a decisive end to the battle. Hannibal, fighting in the middle of the lines, gradually fell back, yielding ground to the superior Roman infantry. The Romans, sensing victory, pressed the attack. One can imagine a young Roman infantryman, seeing the Carthaginians fall back, overcome by the emotion of battle and adrenaline as he lets out his battle cry, pressing the attack and his subsequent astonishment to see the Carthaginian cavalry smash into the rear of the Roman formation from each side.

Hannibal's ruse worked. As the Romans pressed forward in the center of the lines, Hannibal's army encircled the Romans in a crescent shape. His cavalry on each flank quickly defeated their Roman counterpart and supported by battle-hardened African infantry smashed into the sides and the rear of the Roman formation. The Romans, initially sensing victory, now found themselves fighting for their very lives, enveloped by enemy forces on every side. Desperately, although figures vary, about 20,000 were able to fight their way to safety in a nearby town. Hannibal's losses turned out to be a very modest 10,000 or so.

At Cannae, Hannibal accomplished the first recorded double envelopment in military history and the results were profound. The battle rendered the Roman Army essentially combat-ineffective and the political ramifications echoed throughout the Roman Empire for decades. Most military forces lack the operational agility to achieve a flanking maneuver, one of the most difficult maneuvers to accomplish. Yet, Hannibal rolled up not one, but both flanks of a numerically superior enemy and as a result, decimated the Roman Army.[1] Cadets at the United States Military Academy study Cannae to this day as a textbook example of a double envelopment.

The Scourge of Cannae

WHILE shopping in Walmart in Leavenworth, Kansas a number of years ago, I observed a woman who was under a massive spiritual attack, a double envelopment, and likely did not even realize it. Very overweight, the woman couldn't walk; she had to drive one of those little scooters around. In addition to her weight, she just *looked* very unhealthy. She had gray hair, matted and stringy, pulled back into a short pony tail. Her yellowish tinged skin hung sallow and sunken. She looked very ill. Her shopping buggy contained all manner of typical American cuisine, fast, easy, and dare I say poisonous, but what stood out to me was her bag of pills. She had a large bag of prescription pills from the pharmacy, at least five or six different bags. The bottles rattled loudly as she sat them on the conveyor belt.

Instantly, I imagined this poor woman returning to her home, hobbling inside, perhaps with the aid of a walker or cane, heating up a microwave dinner, popping some of her prescription narcotic pain pills or her antidepressants, or both, plopping into her comfortable old recliner, and turning on the television for several hours of oblivion. Granted, I didn't know this woman, had never met her. I based my speculations, my conjecture, solely on a few observations. The reality likely differed greatly from what I imagined to be true, but I couldn't help but think of Cannae.

As I pointed out earlier, throughout much of the world, Satan wages a full frontal assault against God's people. The enemies of God will put you in jail, cut off your head, persecute your family, have you fired from your job, disgrace your honor, banish you, exile you, all for professing the name of Jesus.

The Islamic world is entirely hostile to Christianity as is Communist China, much of Hindu India, and atheistic Japan. In these parts of the world, one cannot doubt that Christians are in a fight for their very lives. Visible and obvious, the forces of evil persecute believers with aplomb. No matter how subtle one may try to be, it would be very difficult to surreptitiously cut off someone's head. People tend to notice these kinds of things.

Yet, the Church absolutely thrives in many of these places. House churches thrive in China; experts predict that they will within a generation consider China a Christian nation. Underground churches grow in Iran, Saudi Arabia, even North Korea. Throughout the history of Christianity, wherever people persecute the Church the harshest, the most blatantly, Christianity thrives. Persecution purifies the Church.

Beginning with the stoning of the first deacon Stephen, recorded in Acts 7, and continuing for the next three centuries, the Roman Empire desperately attempted to extinguish the movement. Nero, Domitian, Trajan all issued edicts calling for varying levels of official persecution. Persecution became policy. Though sometimes limited in scope, several of the edicts declared a universal persecution. As Hebrews puts it:

> Some men were tortured, not accepting release, so that they might gain a better resurrection, and others experienced mockings and scourgings, as well as bonds and imprisonment. They were stoned, they were sawed in two, they died by the sword, they wandered about in sheepskins, in goatskins, destitute, afflicted and mistreated. The world was not worthy of them. They wandered in deserts, mountains, caves and holes in the ground.
>
> Hebrews 11:35b-38

Clearly becoming a Christian in the early days of the church was a largely dangerous affair and yet, the Church exploded throughout the empire. Paul wrote the book of Romans to the church in, well, Rome, within a generation of the death of Jesus. Contemplate that. Within thirty years of the death of Jesus, an established church existed in Rome, the very seat and source of official persecution. Ironically, amazingly, the persecution actually caused or enabled the spread of the Gospel. Paul records the outbreak after the stoning of Stephen.

> And Saul was there, giving approval to his death. On that day a great persecution broke out against the church at Jerusalem, and all except the apostles were scattered throughout Judea and Samaria.
>
> Acts 8:1

Early in Acts chapter 1 and Matthew chapter 28, Jesus commissioned the apostles to "make disciples of all the nations" to go to "Jerusalem, in all Judea and Samaria, and to the ends of the earth". To this point, the Church remained largely confined to Jerusalem as the believers, in their disobedience, wouldn't leave the familiarity of the city. God had said to go, spread the Gospel, but the Church had not obeyed to this point.

So God, in His unsearchable ways, used persecution to spread the Gospel to the point where, by the early fourth century, the emperor Constantine issued the Edict of Milan legalizing Christianity. Before the end of the century, the government declared Christianity the official religion of the Roman Empire.

Similarly, the Bible itself stems from persecution. Early heresies, many taught under the influence of persecution, corrupted the pure teachings of Jesus. So the Church began to gather the authoritative writings of the church fathers into a single collection, the canonization of the Bible into the 66 inspired books. Contrary to popular belief, no Council, no leader, no Edict established the books of the Bible. By the time anyone formulated a list — generally speaking scholars credit the heretic Marcion with the first — the books of the Bible were already in nearly universal usage by the Church, writ large.

Persecution purifies the church and the more intense the persecution, the more purified the church becomes. Yet, the Enemy battles as doggedly as he does deceptively.

As the spiritual battle for the souls of all mankind plays out, Satan clearly employs a different tactic in the west. In the spirit of Cannae, he abandoned the frontal assault and even now, envelops our flanks. Though we may charge headlong into battle and see the enemy retreat before us, if you listen, you can hear the clamor of battle on our exposed flanks. The subtlety quietly resonates, to the point where most Americans do not even realize that a battle rages. Most are content to live out their existence without even realizing that the enemy approaches, just out of sight, on the periphery.

Subtlety

***HAVE** you ever been through a choke point?* To continue with the military meme, a checkpoint is a constrictive terrain feature that channelizes an element into a smaller area where they become easier to engage. Think of it like a funnel. The ideal place to set up an engagement area and ambush the enemy is where the terrain forces the enemy into a confined area thus making it easier to engage them.

So, have you ever been through a choke point? No, you say. Well, I will contend that if you have been through the checkout counter at Walmart or any other store, you have been through a choke point. If you want to buy something prior to leaving Walmart, you have no choice but to go through one of the checkout lines, so not only does it channelize you physically, more than that, it channelizes you for a spiritual assault, a spiritual ambush.

Consider what you may encounter while checking out at Walmart. None of this seeks to demonize Walmart for you can find the same thing at just about any store, but just to make an example. Think back to the last time you went through the line. What did you see? First, you are assaulted with all manner of impulse buy of things that are physically bad for you: candy, gum, soda, cigarettes and tobacco in some of the lines, energy drinks, chips, all manner of things that are bad for the temple, the body. Look deeper.

Think of the publications you can peruse. You can read about the latest sex tips while waiting in line. You can read about the sex moves that will drive your man wild. You can see who had sex with whom. You can read about and see pictures of the best and worst beach bodies. You can peruse near-pornographic pictures of incredibly scantily clad women. Your kids can look at all of these things along with you.

Think about the man standing in line with his rather ordinary looking wife. Maybe he has a lust issue or struggles with pornography. Every single time he goes through the checkout line at Walmart, he has an opportunity to lust, to commit adultery in his heart against his wife.

Consider a young overweight lady. Ironically, her weight issues may possibly stem from consuming the very items that reside in the choke point. She struggles with body image issues and every single time she goes through the checkout line at Walmart, she gets reminded that she does not look like she should, that she should look differently if she wants to be desired. She does not look as she should.

Consider the young men and women who are reminded every single time they go through the checkout line that premarital sex is not just okay, it is practically expected. Maybe they just aren't doing it right. Who could possibly expect you to abstain until marriage?

I had an encounter once with the manager of the Shoppette on Fort Leavenworth, Kansas. Right at about the eye level of a toddler, the store had placed a magazine on the rack that celebrated the derriere of well-endowed women. Yes, such a magazine exists. I complained vehemently to the manager and wrote some letters. Eventually they put up one of those black plates that obscures the cover, but the magazine stayed.

Subtle, yes. Effective, definitely. Satan methodically does to western Christians what Hannibal did to Varro at Cannae, forgoing the frontal assault in favor of attacking the unprotected flanks. Just as at Cannae, the double envelopment, the flank, the subtlety of Satan's assault upon the west devastates equally if not more than the frontal assault that takes place elsewhere around the world. Satan uses chemical addiction as a key weapon upon the flanks of the unsuspecting.

Equipped with the weapons of chemical addiction, alcohol, drugs and prescription medication, Satan envelops this nation, defeating us in a battle that we don't even know about, a battle that most of us are not even fighting. Most will readily acknowledge that *illegal* drugs are bad, though even that metric changes almost daily, particularly concerning marijuana. Let's consider for a moment though *legal* drugs, those found in prescription medication.

Consider that the United States makes up roughly 4.6% of the world's population but consumes 80% of the world's opioids and 99% of the world's hydrocodone, the active drug found in Vicodin, the most popular pain killer. Prescription drug use and abuse continues to skyrocket. In 2006, doctors prescribed 112 million doses of Vicodin. In 2011, it was up to 131 million doses, most of which are, according to more than a few doctors, absolutely unnecessary, medically speaking.[2] Do some cursory research and see for yourself. Ami told me once that I would be surprised how many people we knew, specifically women, were on prescription pain pills or antidepressant and she was right.

This does not surprise me given our current stance as a society. Solve your problems; take a pill. Instead of addressing the cause of pain and making a change or an adjustment to a lifestyle, take a pill. Self-gratification and relief are the order of the day. According to the CDC, prescription drug abuse deaths now exceed the deaths caused by crack cocaine in the 1980's.[3]

This is an epidemic of the highest order. Prescription narcotics, essentially legal heroine, do not frequently solve problems. They numb, they dull, they anesthetize, they addict, they enslave, just like any other chemical and if you are under the control of a narcotic, legal or otherwise, you are not under the control of the Holy Spirit.

Carolyn, 41, from New York, typifies the progression. Years of playing the violin left her with chronic shoulder pain. At the age of 26, an unscrupulous doctor of course prescribed her Vicodin. As her body developed a tolerance for Vicodin, she required progressively more powerful pain pills. Her addiction progressed to the point where she lost her teeth, sold her violins, and began forging prescriptions to feed her addiction.[4]

This is a scourge, a legal scourge, but a scourge nonetheless. There should be only shame for doctors who prescribe first, being reluctant to actually address the actual issues, succumbing to demands for instant relief. Often, both physically and spiritually, pain serves as an indicator, a symptom, a warning of an actual condition that needs to be addressed. If something dulls the pain or renders the person numb to the pain, then the actual condition will persist.

I have a special affinity for prescription antidepressants. Do you know what one of the major side-effects of antidepressants is? Suicidal tendencies! Am I the only one who sees some lunacy, insanity even, in this notion? I am depressed because of a chemical imbalance so I will take a pill that may cause me to have suicidal tendencies. I can think of fewer more satanic notions than this.

At 18 years of age, Joe came to our home as a part of a ministry my wife and I run. He had a somewhat typical foster kid's life, moderate abuse by a birth parent, abandonment. Somehow Joe managed to finish high school and then proceeded to mope around the house for several months. My wife and I encouraged him to get a job to take some steps, but he would just mope around, grouchy, obviously down in the dumps, feeling sorry for himself.

He also had a physical issue but we discovered that he had insurance through his father, so we encouraged him to get the condition checked out, which he did. During the examination, he mentioned to the doctor that he was depressed and that shameless doctor prescribed Zoloft. No blood-work, no consult, no follow-up with a behavioral health specialist. Here are your pills, now go home and watch television.

On the ride home from the doctor, I asked him how it went. He pulled out the pills and said, “Well, at least I got these.” I told him that he ought to take them home and flush them down the toilet. I explained to him that he wasn’t depressed that he was just not living out God’s intent for man which was to work, to be productive, to get out and live and experience the world. I continued to explain that he was just in a funk from lying around the house living a pointless existence. Two weeks later, he actually got a job and his spirits changed dramatically, instantly. Nothing cures “depression” like an honest day’s work. He soon found himself too tired to be depressed and he forgot all about Zoloft. Again, we should heap nothing but shame upon doctors who flippantly prescribe antidepressants.

According to the federal government, nearly 1 in 10 Americans takes prescription antidepressants. Nearly ¼ of women in their 40’s and 50’s take antidepressants, an astounding number. One in four! Less than a third of those taking antidepressants receive the care of a mental health professional.[5] Zoloft, Prozac, Zanax: antidepressants do the same thing that pain pills do: dull, numb, enslave.

Perhaps the scariest notion is that we are collectively raising a generation of prescription drug addicts to carry on the tradition. These days, putting a kid on Ritalin or something else to combat ADD or ADHD is a given. Increasingly, doctors are prescribing toddlers ADHD medicine. We just do it, with very little consideration and doctors push it. Increasingly parents allow their children to be placed on antidepressants or even antianxiety drugs and many psychotropic or psychiatric drugs are decidedly dangerous.

A recent article written by the Citizens Commission on Human Rights (CCHR International) reveals that almost all mass shootings in recent years have one unifying factor and no, it’s not the presence of guns. In each of these cases, the shooter had a prescription for some form of psychotropic or psychiatric medication, be it Ritalin, Zoloft or something else.[6] The side-effects of these medications are often mania, psychosis, hostility, aggression and homicidal ideations. We introduce and addict our very children to these same drugs.

An Acceptable Scourge

I do not want to impugn those who actually suffer from depression or some sort of chronic pain that actually requires medication. Certainly depression and chronic pain are an issue and cases exist where prescription drugs are appropriate. I personally understand the mentality, the thinking, the desire for relief.

I had reconstructive knee surgery in 2010 and for a number of years, my knee worked fine. Shortly after the New Year in 2014 though, it started coming apart. An MRI confirmed that the original repair was fraying and the cartilage was damaged throughout. The orthopedic surgeon confirmed that I needed a new knee, but was just too young. I became miserable, depressed, as I was not able to do the things I wanted to do anymore. What if I could have a pill to make it stop hurting, so I could do the things I wanted to do? It would be incredibly tempting. I truly understand the desire for relief from pain.

Yet, the statistics bear it out as does the reality of the people I know. Many turn to a pill to cope, to deal with life, to deal with stress instead of relying upon that which can be relied upon. Satan's effectiveness in enslaving a generation to prescription pain medication reverberates in the fact that very few people even recognize it as an issue, subtlety again being the order of the day.

Hey, I don't have to go to the corner dealer to get chemicals to alter my brain function, I can simply go to my doctor and tell him that I have chronic pain or that I am depressed and I guarantee that I will go home with a pill of some kind. Think of the public figures that have come out as addicted to prescription meds. I guarantee that you know someone enslaved to prescription meds. Maybe they enslave you.

The enemy's options with respect to chemical affliction range along the scale of acceptability or legitimization. Prescription medication lies at the furthest end of the scale. They are prescribed by a professional, a doctor no less. How could they be bad? They treat valid medical conditions. Alcohol, perfectly acceptable and even expected on certain occasions, resides just a bit further down the scale but remains entirely in the range of acceptability. However, most will acknowledge that there are those who do abuse alcohol. Marijuana registers in the neighborhood of alcohol on the scale. I foresee a time when most will consider it more acceptable than even alcohol. These three (prescription medication, alcohol, and marijuana) exist collectively in a circle of societal acceptability.

Yet, though they may be acceptable or legitimate, that does not diminish their inherent danger and in fact, renders them as dangerous if not more. The spiritual battle rages around each and every one of us, every single day. Because you are unaware or don't acknowledge this fact, it doesn't make it any less true.

Just as at Cannae, Satan enslaves and afflicts, scourging people without conducting a frontal attack. He rapidly rolls up the flanks of an unsuspecting nation, chemical addiction being but a tool to aid in the enslavement. The destruction cuts a widening swath across the core of western society, touching nearly everyone. I pray that we would open our collective eyes to the blight, to the Scourge, to Satan's indirect assault upon the soul of this nation.

CHAPTER 9 DISCUSSION

THIS chapter speaks to the cunning nature of our enemy as a Christian. Read John 8:44. John refers to the Devil as "the father of liars" and a "murderer from the beginning".

1) Where do we see examples of the nature of the Devil in the Bible as "the father of liars" and as a "murderer from the beginning"?

2) Where do you see examples of this in contemporary society?

3) Have you ever personally been deceived by the Devil? When did you realize it? How?

4) Reflect on your current life. Are you being deceived in any way? Are you vulnerable to deception? Why?

Read 2 Corinthians 11:14. Paul mentions Satan as an "angel of light" in the context of false teachers.

5) Is there another context for Satan as an "angel of light" relevant to the context of this chapter.

6) Do you know someone afflicted by prescription pain medication or antidepressants? Do you agree that prescription medication abuse is as dangerous as illegal drug abuse? Why or why not?

Chapter Ten

Brother Joe

SIMILAR to Laurel, much of Joe's past resides in a murky haze of fractious memories. Events and people blur together. If you drink, if you party, you've probably had a night out that you can recall only in bits and pieces. You've had a night whereby you don't recall exactly what happened. Now, imagine that as your life. Imagine living that way for years and you'll begin to understand.

Brother Joe Bradberry is a great man of God, a student of God's Word, faithful to live out God's call upon his life. This hasn't always been the case. My first pastor introduced me to Joe a number of years ago, but it wasn't until God called us both to be a part of a church plant, a new church, that I really got to know him.

A taller, hefty man with soulful eyes and a quick wit, Brother Joe has become one of my best friends and my confidant in Christ. Yet, it wasn't for a number of years that I began to realize his story was atypical of the *perceived* average Christian tale, yet typical and similar of so many other tales of addiction and heartache and affliction. Under the veil, behind the curtain, lay a wasteland of broken dreams, empty promises, and heartache. Yet, his story trumpets redemption, real and tangible redemption, redemption found only in Christ. Just ask him, he'll gladly tell you.

As we talked one Saturday at Lasater's over coffee, I started with a question, "Where did you get your first drink?"

He had a brother who lived in Nashville where he and his niece stayed most summers once school was finished. Joe's brother was an alcoholic, well rapidly on the way to becoming one anyway, and he always had alcohol around: Wild Turkey, moonshine, Budweiser, and Joe and his niece would give it a try. He was around 14, had been a professing Christian for two years, and didn't really care for it much. Seems he hadn't developed a taste for it just yet. That would come in due time.

In retrospect, the providence of God emanates from Joe's life, particularly in dealing with his parents. This came full circle in spiritual life, physical affliction, and physical death. Joe was a preacher's kid. His dad preached at a small, nondenominational country church in Elkton, Kentucky. They had about 30 members or so and one night in 1982, as his dad faithfully preached Christ and Him crucified, which he faithfully did every single time he preached, Joe was saved.

As his father spoke of sin and repentance and man's responsibility to believe, the conviction of his sin came upon him. For the first time, Joe became aware of his sin condition which had separated him from God. A friend of his had been saved previously and couple of other folks professed faith that night but before this day, Joe had never been aware of his own wickedness, the blackness that resided in his heart.

As he spoke of these things, Joe's eyes glazed over as he recalled his meanness of heart and spirit prior. He tortured animals, hated people, hated himself but that night, after calling out to Jesus Christ to save him, he was overcome by an overwhelming sense of peace and calm that he had never experienced before. This well of emotions, the sheer power of God moving through him, drove him to repentance. God gave him a new spirit and then peace. It was as if he had set down an enormous weight that he had been carrying, a burden he had shouldered for so long, and just like that, the weight was no more, the burden relieved.

Joe and his friend Jason got baptized a couple of months later and immediately, Joe began going back to people he'd been mean to, to ask for forgiveness, especially his sister-in-law, who had been the main target of his hatred. A professing Christian, she immediately forgave him. Other things changed as well.

He loved the Lord, began being respectful to his teachers, going to Sunday school, truly loving his neighbors as himself, scarcely recognizing the work of the Holy Spirit. His teen years were in his words, "not too bad," even "uneventful". He did well in school, not great and his parents kept a watchful eye, loving and discerning. They paid close attention to where Joe went, who he was hanging around with, what he listened to. One particular incident stands out as the assault on Joe's flanks began in earnest. He was 16 years old.

Beginning to Stray

JOE had a particular cassette of some heavy metal music that his mother definitely did not approve of. She expressed disappointment, as did his father and warned him that it would warp his mind. The world had begun to steadily entice him. He visited his brother in Nashville more regularly, staying up late watching R-rated movies, trying alcohol. His brother knew, but never told his parents. The world truly started to taste good. He stopped studying his Bible, though his parents were constantly encouraging. Anything that was not of Christ, not of God, began to have more and more of an appeal. He drifted steadily and obviously, not unnoticed by his parents.

Nominality was the order of the day. Church and Sunday School was more than enough. As a spiritual infant, the taste of the world pushed him into conflict as Joe began to rebel against those who loved him the most, his parents. His anger, his frustration and eventually his hatred toward them grew. Joe had to drop out of high school and take a job as a painter to help pay the bills, put food on the table. His father's measly income from the small country church just didn't provide.

How could this be right? How could this be what God wanted? His father served God and look at the results: not even enough money to feed his family. That coupled with the fact that his parents fought, argued intensely, began to cause him to question the goodness of God. Eventually his anger at his parents became anger at God. *He was a Christian, why was he struggling? Why weren't they living the good life as he thought they should?*

As he drifted from God, the world drew him in. Materialism. Wealth. He had to have these things. He owned a used car, but even that wasn't good enough. He wanted a new car, so he went and bought a new Nissan 240SX, loaded. His dad advised him not to calling it a waste of money, encouraging Joe to save his money, put it toward something better, something worthwhile. Joe had a car, but that wasn't good enough, at least in his mind. He sought fulfillment in things that just do not fulfill. As he was learning first hand, you can have the greatest car, the best vacation, the nicest home, but something better always beckons. Joe longed for these things.

> Addictions arise from desire. Desire's main goal is to desire. That's why we need Christ. The Holy Spirit of discipline will keep us from this chase. The yearning needs to be fed. Only Christ satisfies this yearning.

One fateful day, Joe ran into Brian. They used to go to school together and then at the Record Bar in the mall, they ran into one another for the first time in several years. By this time, Joe's soul overflowed with anger, hatred, and animosity towards everyone, most of all himself. He had drifted, far. Thrash metal music — Pantera, Cannibal Corpse, Slayer, Deicide — had replaced God's Word in his life as he became intensely enamored with that which does not fulfill. Brian liked the same kind of music.

> I listened to that stuff out of spite, to hurt the Lord, to hurt my parents.

Joe found a kindred soul in Brian. They struck up a conversation and a friendship ensued based upon a mutual affinity for the same kind of music. Brian asked Joe if he wanted to go to Lollapalooza, the trendy concert series from the mid-nineties. Joe said absolutely, yes, and go he did. They even had beers on the way. It was 1991, maybe.

By this time, though Joe had abandoned his brother in Nashville, he continued drinking. Yet, he had never drank like he did at Lollapalooza. This was really the first time he had been actually drunk. His brother used to like to watch Joe and his niece get tipsy and act silly. He thought it was hilarious. But here at the concert, with the roar of the music, hanging out, seeing other friends he didn't really know, seeing that they were into marijuana, this was different. Joe, drunk at Lollapalooza, got high for the first time. He liked it.

His drift into the haze began in earnest.

Immersion

HENCEFORTH, as Joe immersed himself into the party scene his circle of friends gradually expanded as did the availability of venues for alcohol and drug consumption. One of his friend's parents moved to Dover, over an hour away, and left the house to their two boys. This became the place. Everyone hung out there, the brothers, the friends, girls, everyone. There was always stuff there, always.

Joe had another friend who lived in the basement of his parent's house. As they were always gone, Joe and his friends partied there. In that basement he first tried acid, the genesis for several years of regular acid consumption. Joe spiraled deeper into the abyss as he sought alcohol, week, and acid on a continuous and escalating basis.

> I had many conversations with people who were pot smokers and asked, 'is marijuana a gateway drug?' They would always say, 'no.' I would say, 'yes'. The same people who said 'no', their reasoning was inconsistent. My reasoning was not good, but it was true. I recognized that it wasn't right, that it was irrational, that it didn't benefit. I couldn't explain why it was wrong then though I was putting it before good, seeking fulfillment in things that cannot fulfill.

Binge became life. Weekend pleasure became weeklong pleasure. Everyday. It was something to do. Joe became immersed in selfish distorted thinking, covering up his conviction, dissipating the conviction, numbing himself to conviction, with all different manner of substances.

Joe recollected the first time he tried cocaine. As the spiral continued, he was bound to hit rock-bottom at some point. One particular evening, looking to party, Joe came to the brother's home, but this time, they had locked the doors and wouldn't answer or let anyone in. Joe knew they were there. Undeterred, he went to a nearby gas station and called the house. His friend Jeff answered. Joe wanted to know what they were doing, he wanted to hang out. "We're doing some stuff," was Jeff's response. Reluctantly, he agreed to let Joe in.

Shortly, Joe found himself with the two brothers, Jeff and maybe another guy or two and cocaine. He asked himself, "Do I want to do this?" He had heard about how bad cocaine was for you and so he asked if it was okay, seeking comfort and assurance. "Can it hurt me? Can it give me a heart attack?"

They said, "No, it's okay." Joe rationalized, why not. They're doing it and they're okay. They chopped him a line.

> I snorted it and I really didn't feel anything after that but it felt good. I had found a high to chase. Anyone with an addiction will know what this means. The first high you get when you're stable, when your body is stable, that point is the best step, the first step, and you'll never get that first step again and so you are chasing it, chasing more of that. Now you're closer to it, but you need more to get that feeling, and it starts stressing your body out.

On cocaine:

> Almost like, it races the heart, the blood pressure, just a shot of adrenaline, intensifies everything … I liked it.

Though difficult to find, cocaine became Joe's new thing. He liked it. He began to hang out with the two brothers even more, finding the right people, getting the right hookups, his immersion becoming ever more complete: alcohol, weed, acid, cocaine.

Amazingly, Joe continued to live at home during this tumultuous time but he became increasingly rebellious and hostile. He was disrespectful, didn't follow his parent's rules. His parents knew things were not right, knew that Joe was hurting, knew that he was not seeking after God. Joe said things to his mother, trying to hurt her. In spite of this, his parents never asked him to leave. Joe finally decided on his own to move out, but quickly discovered the harshness of life on the outside. He moved back in just as quickly.

Still using, he would stay up all night playing video games until one night, he met a girl and brought her home. His parents also served as foster parents and at this time, they had two foster children, boys.

When Joe's dad found out about the girl, he went ballistic. Joe had tried to be sneaky, but he knew. Indeed, he had known all along, so he issued Joe a warning. He was not to bring alcohol or girls into the house. He had disrespected his father. "If it happens again, you're out. You can live on the street. If you want to do that stuff, do it somewhere else." Joe stayed.

He continued to do cocaine regularly. One particular day, a day like any other but one destined to be pivotal, a friend introduced him to crack. As Joe played cards with some friends, right down the road from the two brothers' house, he got the taste for a hit. He went to the two brothers' house, searching. Again, they had locked the doors, closed the blinds. Joe, knowing they were home, knocked on the door.

Again, they were "doing something" they told him, "something new." They were smoking crack and since Joe was their friend, they gave him some. He smoked it. It tasted weird, so he smoke some more. They handed him a *primo*, a joint laced with crack. Joe smoked it too. Not wanting to waste any, they put the ashes in an empty beer can, dented the can, poked holes in it, and smoked them as well.

Initially, Joe got mad; he hadn't wanted to smoke crack and they didn't tell him what was in the joint. He confronted the brothers and an argument ensued so they offered Joe another hit. He took it. He had already smoked some, so he smoked some more. Why not? It was 1996 or 1997 and just like that, he became a regular crack user.

Then, it happened again at home, Joe brought home another girl. She smoked and left her ashtray out. Joe's mother found it and as a loving mother, kept it from her husband, so he wouldn't throw Joe out, but he wanted to do these things. Joe wanted to have the freedom to do these things. It was better to leave, so he moved back out.

Joe continued to smoke crack, but he always had a special love for cocaine. They would cut cocaine with baby laxative to spread it out, make it go further, get more money when they sold it. The harder the cocaine, the more pure it is. The more soft and crumbly, the more it has been cut. That's what Joe liked, cocaine. That's what he loved. That's what he wanted to do. Joe had found his drug of choice.

It was during this time that Joe became immersed in pornography. The Scourge opened a new front, but at least he was working, having secured a job at Tennessee Ironworks. One guy warned everyone at work not to talk to Joe in the morning, that Joe wasn't a morning person, not realizing that Joe would be in the midst of a two to three day cocaine binge, many times not having slept in as many days. Joe frequently snorted cocaine during breaks at work. He became increasingly numb to the world, numb to the pain. He snorted so much cocaine that he stopped feeling much of anything. He was dying inside, a little bit every day, maybe even dead already, chasing the high that would never be there. He began to drown his despair in pornography.

Perhaps a vestige of his upbringing remained, but Joe always maintained a certain respect for women. They would have told you that, the girls. Safe to be around, Joe was a good guy. There were always women around and Joe took care of them. He hid them when they passed out, protected them from the wolves. Joe could've taken liberties many times but he never did, not once.

> I thank God that he never allowed me, never allowed me to take advantage of these girls. Lots of them did have things done to them, but I thank God that he didn't allow me to go that deep into that sin. He restrained it to a certain extent.

But he looked at pornography, mountains of it. He drowned in it. Joe had magazines, tons of magazines, magazines that degraded women with the desires of his mind. He had found yet another outlet for the gratification of the flesh. The scar tissue on his soul continued to build.

> I kept going deeper and deeper into fulfilling the flesh, trying to fulfill the flesh. It can't be fulfilled. The flesh is a gulf, not directed by God. The man who does not seek God cannot control his flesh, I don't care who you are, if you're a Christian or not.

About this time, God threw Joe a lifeline and sent a brother. Through it all, Joe continued to work, to live on his own, to struggle. One day at Tennessee Ironworks, a friend named Todd James said to Joe, "You need to get back in church. You need to go to Hilldale. They've got a single's group." As it turns out, Joe needed a much sterner push.

That Day

SEPTEMBER 16th, 1999, was a day that would resonate through the rest of Joe's life. They flipped iron rails that day on heavy horse. After painting one side, Todd would help him flip it to the other. They must've weight several hundred pounds. As he flipped one, Joe's lower back popped and something starting burning, instantly. Something was wrong, but Joe continued to work. That Friday, as he sat in a chair drinking at a buddy's birthday party, his legs started cramping like he had a charley horse. "Why does my leg hurt," Joe thought. So he got drunk, not recognizing this new affliction that continues to haunt him to this very day, his very own thorn in the flesh.

The next Monday, he called his doctor and they sent him to a back specialist who diagnosed him with a bulging disc. The doctors told him he would be okay, that he was overweight, that he needed physical therapy, but that he would be okay. Go figure, they gave him pills. They gave him lots of pills, Mepergan, Percocet, and Joe quickly discovered that he liked them. He liked them even more with alcohol, plenty of alcohol.

On top of it all, Tennessee Ironworks wanted him to sign papers saying that he wouldn't sue. Joe refused. He had worked there for nearly 11 years, had painted lots of railings, for the

Wildhorse Saloon, Alan Jackson, other celebrities. It wasn't right. Joe felt betrayed so he decided to quit, get an easier job.

About the time of the great tire controversy, Bridgestone hired Joe. At this time, lots of heavy litigation swirled about amidst claims of faults found in Bridgestone tires. The work was supposed to be quick, but not strenuous. Yet, because of cutbacks due to the litigation, Joe found himself moving the heavy spools of wire used in the manufacturing process by hand. His back could take no more, the L4 disc collapsed but still Joe continued to work for another three or four months even with collapsed a collapsed disc. He didn't know what else to do.

Joe turned to his pills. He backed off the weed and cocaine and began to take massive amounts of prescription narcotics. He developed a preference for a pill chased with a White Russian - vodka, milk and Kahlua. He drank them religiously. Back then, prescription narcotics were even easier to obtain and after all, they seemed beneficial. They helped his back, so distorted was his thinking. He smoked some, but stuck mainly to his pills and White Russians. The haze thickened.

After nearly six months and lots of pain, Joe could hardly walk. He could only go to the bathroom, bed, kitchen, and couch. He couldn't drive. He couldn't work anymore. His insurance company cancelled his policy. Tennessee Ironworks and Bridgestone disputed where he got injured. This went on for nearly three years. During this time, Joe had two major surgeries along with several outpatient procedures. He lost everything and like that, he had no choice but to go slinking home to mom and dad, hat in hand.

The pace of Joe's descent continued to quicken. His weight ballooned to 360 pounds as he turned to food, eating, sitting around, sporadically in critical care, night terrors, agitated mind, and agitated heart. They gave him more pills, this time for anxiety. He was going to die. In the ICU, they gave him glycerin drops, but they didn't do the job. He eventually turned back to narcotics. They diagnosed him with diabetes. Knowing death was imminent, he had nothing left to live for. This was it. He couldn't work, couldn't sleep. All he could do was hurt.

God had a different idea. Slowly, assuredly, He began to draw Joe back from the edge, back from the abyss.

> When I had met Brian, before I got into hard drugs, we were driving around drinking and I remember looking at him and asking him, 'Why are we here, got to be some reason why we are here'. He changed the subject. All this time, I was still searching. I knew where goodness came from. I knew I wasn't seeking God, His glory. I knew that and every time I was asked to go to church, I'd rail against it. I hated it. I knew this was right. I knew I needed Him. I knew I was seeking what was wrong. That was the constant battle at different points in time.

Back home, Joe finally reached the apex of his descent. He had nothing, but he had God, he still had Christ. After all these years, he had Christ. Despite drowning himself in an ocean of narcotics and alcohol and pornography, despite hating God, despite desecrating all that he knew was right, he still had a Heavenly Father.

They Won't Overcome Me

ONE day, alone at home, he simply asked Jesus to forgive him because he had put all of these things, so many things, in place of Him and he knew all along that they would not fulfill or give peace. He cried out to God and begged Him to deliver, to forgive him for sins, to give peace. Joe hadn't looked at a Bible in some time but he stumbled to his father's study.

"Lord, this is dumb. I cried out to you, I feel like you're here with me. Can you give me something to help me? I don't know a thing about the Bible, even where Jesus died on the cross. Lord, guide my hands as I open this Bible. Give me something." Joe pleaded with tears streaming down his face, as he flipped to the book of Luke and read,

> Look, I have given you the authority to trample on snakes and scorpions and over all the power of the enemy; nothing will ever harm you.
>
> Luke 10:19

All else faded into nothingness in an instant as Joe found himself confronted with the sheer reality of the Word of God. He didn't even know the context of the verse, what it was talking about, but instantly Joe thought, "I have addictions, they won't overcome me. I have diabetes, they won't overcome me. I can have rest in him and no matter what comes against me, **they won't overcome me**."

Joe fell to his knees, crushed by the providence of God, and prayed as he had never prayed before. Sometime later, he arose, changed. That was all it took. It was that simple, this nexus, this crossroads, a mere word from God.

> I didn't tell no one, mom or dad, but they saw it. Mom was like, 'What's wrong with you? You have a peace.'
>
> 'I turned my life back over.' Mom and Dad rejoiced. I repented. It was in that place, that spiral out of control. I had to look toward Him. Hebrews 12. Those God receive He chastises, he allowed me to go through that. He was going to bring me through that. I needed to share this with other people. I can share it. I have taken cocaine, boiled it into crack, in a spoon. I've done all these things. I've broken the antenna off of vehicles to make crack pipes. I've done all these things. That's the power of God, something I'm not ashamed of. This is the healing power to pull us out of darkness. I looked at that verse in Luke 10:19 and I was his disciple and with that calm, I had no more night terrors. I had a peace. I could lay my head down

> at night and sleep and if anything happens to me, I'll be in His presence.

God also offered Joe a chance for redemption with his parents. Shortly after his new commitment, Joe learned that his mother had terminal brain cancer. She lived for another two years, fighting the whole way. Eventually though, she succumbed to the disease. Joe's father died 9 months later. In death came the reconciliation between parents and son that had been needed for so long. So strange to us are the ways of God on occasion. In death comes a newness of life.

Joe cared for both of his parents on their death bed, realizing that it was he who had turned his back on them. They had never turned their back on him. The fighting that they did with one another showed that they were humans. The humble conditions they lived in showed that the good life the world offers is not the life that Christ offers, that the peace in Him was infinitely more gratifying than anything the world could live in. Joe told his dad as he lay dying that he was the best father a guy could ever have. Joe saw his mother go to church with terminal brain cancer to the very last ounce of her strength, witnessing for God in her distress and her affliction, reminding Joe of the old hymn:

> They can have my house,
> They can have my clothes,
> But Jesus Christ has my soul.

In the reconciliation, God changed Joe. He became a different man. Walking his parents to their grave as a loving son served to complete Joe's trip back to the Lord. The joy in the return of the prodigal son must've been abundant. Joe's parents wouldn't have had it any other way.

Looking up from my computer, I realized that Joe and I had been sitting there for several hours. I asked him, "When did you realize you needed help?"

> The whole time I knew. I suppressed it. There was not a time where I acknowledged that, but I always knew, but I refused to turn to Christ, to Him who gives all good things. So, in the end, God allowed me to fall into my own pit, where I couldn't do anything but look up and I knew He drew me back to His loving kindness, mercy, grace, peace ... His love.

Joe had his last back surgery in the 2001/2002 timeframe. He had continued taking the pills for a while, doing a little cocaine here and there but at some point, God made him sick of the drugs. Just like that. He can't even recollect when it happened. It just happened.

> By the power of God, I stopped doing substances. There was a point. I was praying more and more, seeking God more and more, less and less drugs, less and less alcohol. It just kind of happened. I didn't come to a point. It was working in me with the Holy Spirit to move me in that direction. I can't narrow it down to a point. It became even less fulfilling, seeking God became more fulfilling. I was crying out to God. You're all I need. You're all I want. Then I didn't want the drugs. I had wanted them for so long and then I didn't.

Joe started going back to church and for the first time that he could remember, he was happy. He went back to his dad's church. He told everyone that he had repented, that he had turned back to God, that he was professing, that he was walking in truth.

> In that process, I lost a whole person, got down to 232 pounds, through self-discipline that I never had before. God gave me self-discipline. People would see me, knew something was different, wanted to know the difference. I told them that I turned my life back to the Lord. When I shared the power of God with them, it's funny, when I look back, some of the people that I

> thought would be receptive were really hostile. Those who I was worried about, nervous about, scared or tentative to share with, they were receptive. Don't worry about whether they accept or reject, share the truth. That was my joy.

Joe continued to serve at his father's church, but at one point, a friend invited him to Hilldale Baptist Church. It was here that the healing began in earnest. A large Southern Baptist church in the heart of Clarksville, Hilldale had an active and thriving single's group. At their Super Bowl party that year, Joe knew he had found a home.

As he worked through the death of his mother and father, the people of Hilldale reached out and engulfed him with an amazing love. God was his divine support, through the people of Hilldale. There, love overpowered him. He met a man named Garner Griffey, a quiet older man, a farmer. Garner became his mentor. When he spoke, it had power. He didn't waste words on silliness. He met other great folks.

It was at Hilldale that he met Susie.

It was at Hilldale that God called him to preach.

As Joe immersed himself in the Word of God, avenues began opening to teach at Hilldale. One of the pastors told him that he had prayed for a teacher and the Holy Spirit had put Joe on his mind and he couldn't shake the thought. Joe nervously submitted, trusting God, though he lacked any training or education, resting solely upon God, the dispenser of all wisdom.

He still remembers the first time that he went to teach. He asked that pastor to pray for him not to be nervous, not to be scared and to his surprise, the pastor told him that he should be nervous, he should be scared, that he would never pray for that. When handling God's word, realize that you are dealing with matters of eternity. You cannot be lackadaisical. The desire to teach began to bloom in earnest. There was no decision, no point of submission. Joe was led, incrementally, into God's ministry.

Doors opened. Opportunities presented themselves.

Interestingly, a bit of rebellion still remained in Joe's spirit. His parents had given him a Bible and Joe had asked what he should read first. They both said to read the book of John. Never one to submit immediately, Joe said he would pray about it and decided, "I'll get to John when I get to John. I've gotta start at the beginning!" This he did.

Joe sat down with his Bible and began to read, from page one, beginning an incredible journey. For three years, Joe read his Bible. Starting in Genesis chapter 1, verse 1, Joe read. He didn't read other books, seek other guidance, or seek answers elsewhere. Joe studied the Bible

Joe spoke at a friend's funeral. He had studied the book of Matthew and the parable of the talents. "Well done good and faithful servant," Joe preached. He talked about what his friend had meant to the single's group, his compassion. He shared the Word of God.

The desire to proclaim blossomed further.

> An evangelist had come through my dad's church when I was young and he would call people out in church and told them if there was something they were battling or what they had repented of or what God's plan was. He called me after I was saved, called me out in church. God has told me that you are going to be a man after your father's own heart, you will be a preacher, a pastor and I was like, 'yeah, right'. But he was right People had told me they had dreams where I was preaching and I told people that you're crazy, I don't' have a desire.

Joe found the Way. He studied, preached, taught, met and talked with the pastor at Hilldale, Dr. Larry Roberston. He needed something, but didn't know what it was. His girlfriend Susie suggested that he check out the Way, a church plant sponsored by Hilldale. God had led Joe to the new work he needed. Joe knew this was where God wanted him to be. It is at the Way that I met Joe Bradberry again.

> Even though I battle addictions, the temptations are still there. I have a food addiction. I have degenerative disc disease. Lots of things I can't do. I live in pain. Doctors try to give me pills but don't take them. Everything is not a happily ever after. I gained some weight, had other issues, lost weight, but by the grace of God. I lean upon Christ and His mercy and His grace because He promised Paul that His grace is sufficient. We have to lean upon it and as I do that, God gives me the grace I need. Does that mean healing? Maybe. Does that mean whatever his will is? I can seek Him. He is good and just and merciful.
>
> I don't say that what God has done for me, He will do for you. I say repent and believe and He will save you and if by His grace He heals you from your addiction, all glory to Him! I only became aware of the power of the sin I struggled with later in my Christian life. There came an awareness. Part of God's grace is not revealing to us how totally sinful we are.

In October 2013, Joe Bradberry was appointed as a pastor at the Way, a Baptist church in Clarksville, Tennessee. There he continues to proclaim.

CHAPTER 10 DISCUSSION

REVIEW Luke 10:17-20.

1) What are the implications of the authority imbued by God mentioned in this verse?

2) In light of Joe's testimony and your personal experience, what do you say to Jesus' statement "nothing will ever harm you"? To whom was he speaking? What is the context? Is it applicable to us today?

This chapter mentions Joe's story as 'atypical' of most Christian pasts or perceived pasts.

3) Do you believe this to be the case?

4) Is there a typical Christian testimony?

5) Where do you see the sovereignty of God manifest in Joe's life?

6) Do you know a fellow believer in Christ who struggles as Joe did? Have you done anything about it? If so, how did it go? If not, do you intend to?

CHAPTER ELEVEN

Orphans of the Scourge

IT occurred to me that every single foster kid we've had, and I've lost count at 25 or so, has been in the system because of addiction in some manner. Not a single orphan has graced our home, permanently or temporarily, without ties to chemical addiction. *They come because of the Scourge.*

It startles to consider and see firsthand what the addictions have wrought. Even more startling to consider, of all the people we've come to know through the foster system, those who battle the Scourge, only one has managed to get clean and that was Ms. Laurel. All others have succumbed in various ways thus far though I acknowledge that the fight is far from over.

Our very first foster kid, the Little Guy will languish for the rest of his life from the evil effects of his biological mother's decision to abuse chemicals during her pregnancy. Laurel's son Logan lived with us as our second foster kid.

An amazing story of fall and redemption, seeing them now, I easily forget the devastating circumstances surrounding Logan's initial entry into our home. I easily forget the tenuous existence that Laurel lived for the first couple of months and Logan's struggles with being in a strange home, away from his mother. I readily forget the fear and uncertainty when Laurel relapsed for the last time. Yet, as all of that has faded, God has revealed the remarkable though the scars will never completely fade. The scars persist.

A number of children lived with us for whom drug addiction was not the primary reason for their presence in foster care, but the addiction almost always contributes. Physical abuse frequently stems from chemical addiction. Neglect has roots in chemical addiction. In many cases, substance abuse so permeates the fabric of a particular family's existence that it actually defines them. It's there, always present, not outstanding or unusual in any way. It just is. It's what they do and they rarely view life in terms of cause and effect. It's not in their language.

Frequently, they view the *System* as the enemy. They were down on their luck. They couldn't catch a break and though they obviously suffered, the children suffered more. That the connection is rarely made is probably inconceivable to those who are not similarly afflicted. Self-awareness rarely presents itself in those afflicted by chemical addiction, those scourged. Self-denial becomes normative.

I sat in my dining room once and listened to a young lady named Jessie tell me that she actually nurtured her young daughter better when high on marijuana. At 18 years of age, she came to our home from living in her car with her two year old daughter, Josie. Motivated and enthusiastic, at least at first, she got up every day and went to work while we watched Josie. It truly seemed as if she wanted to take advantage of the help that we gave her and the help she got from the *System*.

Inevitably, we began to suspect that she was smoking marijuana. One day, Joe and I sat outside Steak and Shake waiting for her to get off work. Five minutes became ten, then twenty, eventually thirty. She didn't answer her phone, was not in the restaurant. About that time, she came walking from behind the restaurant from another car.

I knew instantly that we were in for trouble and when she got in the car, the smell of marijuana immediately overpowered me. Joe started coughing it was so severe. As I drove her home to her child, I informed her in no uncertain terms that I considered it amazingly irresponsible to get high prior to caring for her child. She apologized, but didn't quite see it that way.

So, we called in the social worker and explained our policy. We are here to help but not enable someone to use. We explained this to her in great detail. Then she informed us that she was a better mother while high and had absolutely no intentions of quitting. This set in motion several weeks of severe drama, the likes of which have not been seen in our household since. Her running away to the streets, stealing Josie from our foster care, high speed car chases (no kidding), animosity, death threats, aggression.

Jessie raged against the world in a way that I hadn't seen before, haven't seen since, and she continued to use the entire time. Eventually, the Department took Josie back from her and brought in Jessie's former foster mother to serve as a kinship emergency placement.

We didn't hear anything from her for over a year until I received a Facebook message from left field. In it, Jessie thanked us profusely for helping, for seeing her through that time. She finally got some behavioral health treatment and some help for her addictions. Whether she can overcome them remains to be seen. Josie still lives in foster care, away from the mother that birthed her.

Justin was the first member of the Clarksville Covenant House. Ami and I both felt led to do something for foster kids who age out of the system without being adopted. For those that are never adopted, statistically speaking, they will fail at life. Addiction, jail-time, homelessness, unwanted pregnancy: all near certainties for foster kids who are never adopted.

The situation is abysmal. System kids all share several common characteristics including a penchant for self-destructive behavior and an inability to see past the next five minutes of life.

It is really quite astounding to witness the commonality.

Anecdotally, they all refer to where they have *stayed*, never where they have *lived*. They have never really lived, I guess, only existed, just *stayed* different places, a very sobering thought.

As such, Ami and I felt led to take those who turned 18 without being adopted into our home to help them get a jump start on life and the Clarksville Covenant House was born. Justin, our first member, confirmed our call to both of us as he nonchalantly strolled into our Sunday School class one Sunday and announced, "Hi, I'm the Grenade" in his Louisiana drawl.

One of the most interesting and unique individuals I've ever met, Justin suffers from the effects of several years of poor decision-making, much of it tied to alcohol and drug abuse. For years, he took pretty much whatever he could get his hands on, but he really liked to drink. He would go to a bar, get drunk, and call AAA to tell them that his car had broken down. When the tow-truck arrived, he'd have his ride home.

Addicts are nothing if not resourceful when seeking to feed the addiction. The end result was not one, but two DUI's for Justin and so he wound up in a court ordered rehabilitation home in Clarksville, a halfway house.

On a side note, Ami and I learned over the years that one of the best places to find drugs is at an AA meeting or in one of these halfway homes. What else would you expect to find when you put a bunch of addicts together under one roof?

It's funny, but that never even occurred to me. I still remember laughing in astonishment as Laurel explained to us how easy one could find drugs or alcohol amongst a group of addicts and how surprised I was to hear that. Why wouldn't a group of addicts likely have addictive substances

Most of these homes and facilities lack much in the way of supervision and many of the tenants reside there court-ordered, against their will.

When Justin finally left the group home, he came to stay with us. He was 24 years old. For several years we worked with him, got him employed full time with a commercial construction company and eventually got him living on his own. It didn't go exactly as planned as he got into a fistfight with another Covenant House kid which spurred us to help him move out, but he was working, living on his own, independent for the first time in his life.

He still struggles. He doesn't use anymore, actively attends church, but has a very difficult road ahead. The financial fallout from a single DUI can overwhelm. The fallout from two can be seemingly insurmountable. Yet he fights, struggles, living the best that he can, going to school now. The light shines from the end of the tunnel and he can see it, but it has been and will be a long road. He just recently got his driver's license reinstated.

D-Win remains one of our favorite guys. A young black kid from St. Louis, Dontae came to live with us at the Covenant House at the age of 18. With an infectious grin and a sweet spirit to go along with his explosive temper, D-Win stole my wife's heart. A rapper like Dewayne, hence D-Win, he too liked his marijuana. D-Win *stayed* with us for over a year and then returned to St. Louis where he descended into the abyss of the drug related scourge.

He used, he sold, he stole to support his habit. He has warrants for his arrest. He got his girlfriend pregnant and eventually got arrested in Atlanta for domestic assault. His daughter currently grows up fatherless, scourged from birth by the demons of affliction.

Scourged from Afar

YOUNG Miguel, our three year old, is without a doubt the orneriest rascal you've met. Cute beyond belief and equally as stubborn, Miguel has thus far avoided life on the fringe. DCS brought him to us over a year ago from intensely tragic circumstances but I need to tell you about Oscar and maybe Gina.

On the surface, these two represent everything that I would otherwise normally loathe. An illegal immigrant and former drug dealer, Oscar works as a day laborer in Nashville. The unmarried mother of three children from two different men living in poverty and a former illegal immigrant, Gina struggles for her very existence and the existence of her children, two of whom are already in state custody, including our Miguel. A recent test confirmed her fourth pregnancy.

I am intensely conservative in my beliefs and politics and I know the answers to the test on this one. Some would cry, "Deport them all! Send them back to Mexico!" Others might demand, "Sterilize her. She has no business having children out of wedlock that she can't take care of! This is not our problem, not what my tax payer dollars are for!"

Yet, I have learned that the canned answers to the test only answer the grade school examination. The graduate exam is an essay test, not multiple choice. The graduate exam comes when you actually know the people and understand that these are real people, living real lives, no different in many ways from you and me. Victims do actually exist. Gina and Oscar have lived a tragic and harsh life until now and unfortunately, their future likely will consist of more of the same.

Both were *brought* to this country at a young age. They did not choose to come here. Gina was brought to Texas and at some point, she must've been about 13 years old, her mother's boyfriend, an illegal immigrant himself, decided that he liked Gina better than her mother. He took her, impregnated her, and brought her to Tennessee. Her daughter still lives in Texas. In Tennessee, he impregnated her again. She had Miguel. Again, just so you realize, I am speaking about a middle aged *man* with a teenage girl. The government actually deported him and Gina came to us as a foster child, with Miguel.

Oscar speaks the most excellent English I've ever seen from an immigrant. He learned by watching television. As he explains it, after being brought to a new and strange country, he literally watched television for 8 to 10 hours a day for months on end. Intelligent, articulate and with a great sense of humor, Oscar somehow managed to finish high school completely on his own. I have no idea how an illegal immigrant can finish high school, but he has his diploma. I find that fact alone simply amazing. Early on, Oscar did what he had to do; he sold drugs, lots of drugs, and he made lots of cash. He did well. Then, he met Gina. They started dating and not surprisingly, he got her pregnant.

It was then that he decided to quit living like he was for the sake of his son. He wanted to live a life of which Oscar, Jr. could be proud so Oscar took a full-time job doing menial labor around Nashville. I asked him how that worked, as an illegal immigrant. Quite simply, there exists a network of illegal immigrants and they all know who doesn't do background checks or who doesn't care. They work for half the pay and because there are always others seeking work, they work very hard just to keep the job. Life has become increasingly difficult and the tragedy of their circumstances has begun to catch up to them. It all started when Oscar got pulled over.

Now the system has a record of him and he must answer in court. Desperately needing legal representation and facing potential deportation, Oscar lacks the several thousand dollar retainer fee for a lawyer. Recently he has pondered a return to Florida for a few months, to scratch together some cash. He ponders the very thing he swore off some time ago, selling drugs again. He still knows his old connections, but it eats at him. He knows that Oscar, Jr. needs him, needs a father, but he desperately does not want to sell drugs. The situation suffocates him and I know he feels tempted just to walk away, just to run. I cannot imagine having to make these types of decisions.

Behind the statistics, people's lives speak loud and clear, tragically. The answers seem cut and dried from afar. It's like flying at 10,000 feet in Afghanistan over some of the most beautiful and magnificent country in the world. It's only when you descend into the fray that you see the chaos and destruction of decades of warfare. Likewise, I challenge anyone to immerse themselves in the actual scourge and then make blanket statements concerning policy and law. Make policy and law after becoming familiar. Though I still consider myself conservative in just about every way possible, my stance has softened significantly on a number of issues as I've seen the *people* and *circumstances*, often tragic in nature, up close and personal. It resonates.

A Local Scourge

OUR newest guys came to live with us last year. I spoke of generational sin earlier as a biblical reality and this last year, Ami and I received a firsthand look at the inner workings of the generational sin of chemical addiction as it ravages successive generations of this particular family. The boys have lived with us for over a year and the scourge of addiction has devastated their entire family - mother, father, sisters, aunts, uncles — all of them.

A stereotypical, backwoods Tennessee meth family, not a single person has not been torn apart in some way by the demons of addiction. One of the sisters even got arrested for running a meth lab in a hotel room. Ami and I pray that the cycle will be broken with the boys. The younger one seems moderately and mercifully oblivious to his plight. The older one, however, though just a teenager, seems to understand that he doesn't stand a chance. He realizes this, resigned to the reality of his existence.

Loyalty tears at both of them, loyalty to a family and culture that they know will destroy them and the potential for a new life, apart from all the familiarity of their previous existence. I cannot imagine being confronted with so serious of a situation at their age. Do you embrace the new way or cling to the familiar, all you've ever known? The older boy recounted how he used to actually run drugs from the inside of a crack house to buyers in cars out front. Both boys remain nearly emotionless about the issue, a disturbing façade suggesting a deeper inner turmoil that belies their outer stoic countenance. I imagine this defense mechanism has served them well as they've bounced from home to home in the foster system for a number of years.

For so many, life on the fringe becomes the norm. Again, for those not enslaved to addiction, this manner of existence seems nearly unfathomable. So many live from hand to mouth, existing solely in the present. I'm not talking about existing in the present the way that God calls us all to live our lives in the present, to be aware of the people and circumstances that He has placed around us so as not to miss those divine opportunities. I am talking about living in the present with no foresight, no thoughts of the future, no consideration of consequences of actions. From our various foster kids to their immediate and extended families, a day-to-day existence is normative. Unashamedly, they rely upon the system that they simultaneously demonize, completely immersed in the sorrow of life and disturbingly unaware of the larger construct of their plight. The lack of awareness troubles me the most, prompts the most questions.

When we take the new guys to see their father for his weekly visitation, he frequently does not even know how he is getting back from the visit. His truck frequently breaks down and so when they finish their visit, he'll start making phone calls and sometimes even start walking. He has been enslaved to chemical addiction for most of his adult life, eking out an uncertain existence amidst the harshness of the daily scrabble. He clearly does not often know where his next meal may come from and he considers this normal.

Our Family

FROM Dewayne, to Joe, to Laurel, to the little guy and so many others, over the course of this work, I have become even more convinced of the desperate conditions that surround us. I have become aware of so many who live life on the fringes, waging a losing battle on their own, clearly not as God had planned for us to live in His revealed will. Yet, this is my family.

Ami and I consider all of our foster children as our children. One of the most difficult questions I am ever asked is, "How many children do you have?" The answer depends upon what you mean by that question. Legally, Ami and I have five children, two from adoption. We are the legal guardians of little Miguel. We consider all of our children as ours, foster and otherwise.

Currently, today, I could answer the question this way, we have nine children. Yet, I would certainly include our Covenant House kids, so maybe it's more. This is my family and they have all been scourged. The demons of chemical addiction have afflicted them for life. Though the effects *may* diminish over time, they will assuredly resonate, enduring for life.

Yet, in all this we've seen the miraculous hand of God at work in our family. We've seen the afflicted give their lives to Jesus Christ, stop using drugs, get jobs, get accepted to college. From the suffering and affliction a certain energy now permeates our family. For the first time for so many, there is hope, hope that rejuvenates, hope that sustains.

Anyone who loves knows the difficulty in seeing one you love suffer, whatever may be the reason for that suffering. Ami and I pray that our family will provide a bastion of relief from this plague of suffering wrought by the Scourge, these demons of chemical addiction and that the hope that is found in Jesus Christ will continue to conform all of us to the glory of His image.

Chapter 11 Discussion

THIS chapter addresses the widespread, familial affliction caused by alcohol and drug abuse.

1) Do you know any families similarly afflicted? Is your family one of them?

2) Is this condition unique to contemporary times? Has there been a progression of this affliction? Reflect on your life and observations.

This chapter also deals with preconceived notions concerning law and policy. In light of that:

3) What are your political/social leanings? Are they biblically based? Why or why not?

4) Do you believe your political/social leanings are grounded in the reality of life on the street?

5) Would it potentially change your beliefs if you or your family were similarly afflicted?

Read Ecclesiastes 1:9.

6) In light of this chapter and this entire book, how do you reconcile the statement that "there is nothing new under the sun" with what you have read?

7) List some afflictions early Christians dealt with that are not as prevalent today?

8) Think of the contemporary afflictions discussed in this book, alcohol abuse, drug abuse, pornography. Are these afflictions apparent in the history of the church?

Conclusion

A Global Issue

ALL suffer under the Scourge in some manner, this blight on the fabric of humanity, the face of our nation. The Scourge has gone global.

Recently, the state of Colorado legalized marijuana. I can think of nothing worse than legalizing yet another substance that disassociates man from reality. A friend of mine recently recounted to me that a family member of his had quit the Army and was moving to Colorado to smoke marijuana for a bit. That's the plan. I'll just move out to Colorado to smoke for a while, until I figure out my next move. I cannot imagine that working out well.

I can only praise God that I never tried a single illegal drug. I drank. I drank a lot, but I never tried drugs, not once. To be sure, this was in no way due to any righteousness within me, but I was always a rule follower, afraid of getting into trouble and since drugs are illegal, I just didn't do them. I hold no elevated view of any type of infallibility within me. It actually frightens me to think of what drugs may have wrought in my own life as I have a very addictive, slightly OCD, type of personality. When drinking, I'd drink with a vengeance and I can easily envision myself consuming cocaine with equal aplomb, now at least. That hasn't always been the case.

There was certainly a time where I looked down upon the afflicted, whereas I even considered them lesser. Yet, over time, as I have drawn closer to Jesus Christ, become ever more aware of my own fallibility, that I am a great sinner, I have seen that I am capable, capable of great transgression. As I have witnessed the broad scope of addiction, I have come to see the afflicted in light of the battle, for what they are, for who they are. I am humbled to see humanity thus afflicted. God has provided me and my family a backstage pass to the scourge of chemical addiction.

We've seen heartache, sorrow, pain, anger, rage. Yet, we've seen triumph, great triumph, and that glory, when contrasted with the bleak backdrop of suffering, radiates joyfully. Where darkness pervades, even the dimmest of lights emanates blindingly. From this darkest of existences, the sordid conditions frequently surrounding the Scourge, the light becomes the *only* thing visible.

The Struggle

LET'S revisit the Struggle. The issue is that the lashing about becomes the struggle. Men become unaware of the burden, so bloodied are their legs. As they stumble and stagger about under the crushing weight of the burden, they only feel the intense pain in their legs from the lashing about. If only the lashing about would stop, then all would be okay. Yet from afar, we see that the burden eventually crushes them all, whether lashed about or not. The lashing about is temporal, the burden crushes eternally, but for those being crushed, the temporal is the only thing realized.

God calls the man of faith, the Minister, to do much more than stand idly by as men are crushed by the burden and the lashing about. Several major issues plague the man of faith as the sheer messiness of the struggle becomes the primary hindrance to engagement. Lives are messy and for those who struggle, those living the struggle, lashed about, lives are excessively messy. Clean and decisive solutions, quite simply, do not exist. Rarely does the phrase *happily ever after* get uttered. The miraculous happens, but it happens according to God's timing, in God's way, and it is almost always, without exception, incredibly messy. If only people would behave as they should when trying to minister to them.

The Minister will soon discover a striking revelation, that many of the burdened and lashed about actually hold the whip in their own hands. *They* are the ones who hold the whip. Satan may have handed it to them but they now have full possession, complete control. It seems that once the lashing begins in earnest, Satan considers his task complete and the burdened will continue to lash themselves. As the man of faith will soon discover, they have been lashing themselves for quite some time. It is what they know to do. They even have come to like it, to be so lashed.

Eventually, the man of faith will find himself also lashed about as he places himself in the way of the lashing. Ministering to those thus stricken will almost certainly lead to a quantity of pain and suffering upon the Minister himself. Rarely, if ever, does the man of faith intervene bloodlessly and you'll soon find that every true Minister bears many scars.

Because of this messiness, time limits engagement serving to constrain involvement. Sheer busyness prevents many from engaging those with the burden, those lashed about. The need always arises when least convenient. When the man of faith, the Minister, sits down for a nice family dinner, he should expect a phone call. When the Minister just drifts off to sleep, he should expect a phone call. When the Minister absolutely has somewhere else to be, the need will almost certainly arise. The need absolutely never happens at an appropriate time.

Lastly, some are so afflicted, so lashed about, so bloody, that the Minister becomes discouraged. The man of faith laments, "What could I possibly do? What difference could I possibly make?"

A proper understanding of the notion of sovereignty, though it won't alleviate these concerns entirely, may possibly render them moot though the true minister can never quite stomach the notion of helplessness. He will never quite get used to the affliction. He will understand, but it will grate at him.

Yet, what of the burden? The lashing about, though an issue, is certainly not *the is*sue. What could we possibly say to men thus burdened? Would they listen if we told them to ignore the lashing about, that it's not what's important? What if we could even stop the lashing about? They will still carry the burden, crushing them as assuredly as before. What if we told them about the burden, that they could merely set it down or perhaps more appropriately, that you know One who will relieve them of it?

Man languishes under the burden of sin, wrought by the Fall of the first Adam. Sin distorts all of reality. The very creation groans under the weight of sin. Though some may be able to live *well* of their own accord, they could never live *righteously*. As a result of the Fall, man requires a Savior.

We have a singular hope, and that hope is Jesus Christ. As every addict I've ever encountered has related to me, no human power can save one from the power of the demons of addictions, from the Scourge. Man, possessing even the most iron of wills, provides no match for a substance that will literally drive mothers to betray their sons, sons to betray their mothers. True healing, healing from the scourge of sin itself, is only found in Christ. Jesus heals and Jesus saves. This is the undeniable truth of Scripture.

Choices

WHAT is your role in the Struggle?

Are you a minister, a man of faith? "What must I do?" is the question I am fervently praying you will ask. The answer is decisively simple. Engage. Engage and let God work out the details. If you have given this work even a cursory skimming, then you know things. You know about the Scourge. I would argue that if you opened your eyes and looked around, really looked, you would become even more aware of the Scourge.

Engage. If you are serious about involvement, prayerfully consider foster care and/or adoption. Contact your local Department of Children's Services or a private agency such as Youth Villages or OmniVision. These places are like triage for those afflicted by the Scourge and I guarantee that they can provide you with some very specific needs. Organizations such as Alcoholics Anonymous or Celebrate Recovery provide innumerable ways to get involved.

Do you personally know someone struggling under the Scourge? Pray for them. Talk to them. Engage them. Support them. Encourage them. Encourage others to engage.

The *what* or *how* of engagement is not nearly as important as the attitude of engagement. Decide to engage and the Lord will certainly lead you in the path He has set for you or you can return to your Iphone and your triple macchiato caramel latte and forget all about any of this unseemly business.

Let's ask a potentially more dangerous question. Are you afflicted yourself? Do you number among the scourged? Do you know the demons of the Scourge personally?

I've struggled with what to tell you because the simple truth is that there is nothing you probably haven't heard before or don't already know. I would be remiss if I didn't reinforce to you that the Scourge is the way of death, that this road you are traveling will certainly end with your destruction. Maybe you have traveled this road for many years or maybe you are just taking your first tentative steps in that direction, but you already know this, don't you?

The relevant question is, "what can you possibly do?" I must return you to the beginning, to Ms. Laurel's account. Reflect upon her, Dell, the others, their struggle, and recognize that, *No Human Power Can Save You.* No human power can save you. You are truly in the clutches of the demonic who seek your literal destruction. All other "steps" become irrelevant in light of this literal and critical acknowledgment.

After this, the ball is in your court. Do you really want to quit or do you like it too much? "Why doesn't God just heal me?" you may ask. Let me reassure you that He can, and He will, but the sovereignty of God is never reconciled with personal responsibility. God holds us accountable for the decisions that we make.

When you pick up that needle, when your friend passes you the joint, when you throw back the shot, you are deciding to destroy yourself. You hold the whip in your own hand. Recognize this. Recognize this and set it down. For the sake of your life, set it down. You still have something to offer this world. Maybe God has a plan to use you in a mighty way if nothing more than to encourage someone else who struggles as you have. Either way, set it down.

Get help. God intends no man to live on an island. Find a clean friend. Go to the nearest biblical church. Find the local AA chapter. Find a Celebrate Recovery chapter. Renounce those in your life who lead you in the Scourge, physically. Walk away, literally. Don't look back. When you fail, get back up and continue the fight but fight you must. Never stop, never. The only other option is imminent destruction. The situation is critical. It is urgent! *Decide.*

Do you still carry the burden?

What I mean by that is do you still languish under the penalty of your inherited sin condition? Do you know Christ Jesus as your Lord and Savior?

Whether you suffer under the Scourge or not, rest assured that true healing only comes through Jesus Christ in healing your very soul. Any struggle is temporal. The Struggle is eternal.

Amazingly, you don't need a priest or even a church. The Bible tells us that if we confess with our mouths that Jesus is Lord and believe in our hearts that God raised Him from the dead, then we will be saved. It's that simple. The Bible tells us to call upon the name of the Lord and He will answer. Confess your sin to Him, acknowledge your utter helplessness, and be saved.

If you feel the Lord stirring in your heart today, even just a bit, let me encourage you to find a Christian friend, find a church, ask questions. Don't be satisfied until you know the Answer.

I surrendered to Christ's call in April 2005. I pray that you would do that today. Pray for healing. Pray for forgiveness of sin. Pray for salvation. I promise you, God does as well, that no human power can save you.

Soli Deo Gloria.

FINAL DISCUSSION

DO you agree with the statement, "All suffer from the scourge in some way, this blight on the fabric of humanity, the face of our nation"? Why or why not?

In light of the struggle spoken about in the introduction and conclusion:

1) Where do you fit into the struggle? Are you burdened, lashed about? Are you the minister?

2) If someone asked you what this burden was and how you would get rid of it, what would be your answer?

3) Where is the struggle most evident in your community?

4) What is your role in the struggle? To where has God called you? What keeps you from engaging in the struggle?

Reflect on the personal accounts in this book along with the commentary.

5) What is the main take-away from this book?

6) Do you agree with the author's primary assertions? Are there major points you disagree with? If so, which ones and why?

7) How can you apply what you may have learned while reading this book?

8) Do you know someone who needs to hear the lifesaving message of the Gospel of Jesus Christ? What is keeping you from telling them?

Personal Note

PERSONAL NOTE

THANK you so very much for taking the time to read Scourge. I pray that you'll consider getting involved.

Do you know that orphans, children with no family, live in your city, available for immediate adoption? Do you know that your local Department of Children's Services is desperate for foster families?

You can make an eternal difference in a child's life. I cannot think of many things more important than that.

In Christ,

Brad

BIBLIOGRAPHY

BIBLIOGRAPHY

Following are references to verses of scripture in the order of appearance.

Ephesians 6:12
1 Peter 5:8
Genesis 3:15
Isaiah 46:9-10
Romans 3:23
Romans 2:1-16
James 2:10
Isaiah 64:6
Isaiah 10:5-7
Psalm 139:1-16
Psalm 8:3-8
Proverbs 20:1n
Proverbs 23:20-21
Luke 21:34a
Romans 13:13
Luke 1:13-15
Proverbs 104:14-15
Matthew 11:18-19
1 Corinthians 8:4-5
1 Corinthians 8:7-12
Colossians 3:16a
James 2:14-26
James 1:22
James 1:27
Luke 4:14
Luke 4:18-19
Exodus 22:21-27
Deuteronomy 24:19-22
James 2:24
James 2:14-19,26

1 Corinthians 5:11

Galatians 5:19-21

Ephesians 5:18

1 Peter 4:3

James 3:1

1 Timothy 3:3

Titus 1:7

Numbers 6:2-3b

Proverbs 31:3-7

Isaiah 5:11

Isaiah 5:22a

Matthew 22:37-40

Matthew 24:3

Matthew 25:31-46

Isaiah 58:1-7

Exodus 34:6-8

Hebrews 11:35b-38

Acts 8:1

John 8:44

2 Corinthians 11:14

Luke 10:17-20

Ecclesiastes 1:9

END NOTES

Chapter One
1. Gendar, Alison. "Nation of Islam mosque killing of NYPD cop still a mystery, 37 years later." *Daily News*, March 22, 2009. http://www.nydailynews.com/news/crime/nation-islam-mosque-killing-nypd-mystery-37-years-article-1.369007.

2. Representative Press. "1998 Fatwa.", http://www.representativepress.org/1998Fatwa.html.

Chapter Eight
1. Wright, Jerome. "Frayser works to get past the jokes and the blight." *The Commercial Appeal,* December 30, 2007. http://www.commercialappeal.com/opinion/on-the-cusp-frayser-works-to-get-past-the-jokes.

2. Haskins, Ron. "Combating Poverty: Understanding New Challenges for Families." Brookings Institute, June 5, 2012. http://www.brookings.edu/research/testimony/2012/06/05-poverty-families-haskins.

Chapter Nine
1. Wikipedia. "The Battle of Cannae." http://en.wikipedia.org/wiki/Battle_of_Cannae.

2. Avila, Jim. "Prescription Painkiller Use at Record High for Americans." *ABC News,* April 20, 2011. http://abcnews.go.com/US/prescription-painkillers-record-number-americans-pain-medication/story?id=13421828.

3. Ibid.

4. Ibid.

5. Rabin, Roni. "A Glut of Antidepressants." *The New York Times,* August 12, 2013. http://well.blogs.nytimes.com/2013/08/12/a-glut-of-antidepressants/?_php=true&_type=blogs&_r=0.

6. CCHR International. "Are psychotropic drugs actually linked to mass shootings?" April 15, 2013. http://www.cchrint.org/2013/04/17/are-psychotropic-drugs-actually-linked-to-mass-shootings/.

ABOUT THE AUTHOR

BRADFORD SMITH has been married to his best friend Ami since 2001 and they stay busy raising their nine children together. A West Point graduate, Brad has served on active duty since 1995 including multiple combat tours to Iraq and Afghanistan.

In 2007, Brad surrendered to the call to preach and in 2011 he joined the staff of The Way, A Baptist Church in Clarksville, as the Missions Pastor where he continues to serve bi-vocationally.

In 2010, Brad and Ami opened the Clarksville Covenant House for teenagers who age out of the foster system and in 2013, Brad graduated from Liberty Theological Seminary with a Masters of Divinity.

Once the Army releases him from duty, he plans to plant a new Baptist church and run the Covenant House full time alongside his wife.

www.thewayofclarksville.com

www.thewayofclarksville.com/covenant-house

MORE TO COME

"No Higher Call"

A Biblical Treatise on Adoption

By Bradford Smith

THE cry of the orphan reverberates across the nation. The fatherless flood our systems and courts in an overwhelming deluge. Every year, 25,000 foster children turn 18 and "age out" of the system without ever being adopted and — for them — the prognosis for the rest of their lives is exceptionally grim. Many face homelessness, imprisonment , poverty, pregnancy out of wedlock, addiction, or violent death.

Meanwhile, the vast majority of American churches stand idly by. No Higher Call challenges American Christians to take action while examining the need and the Bible's surprisingly clear teachings on this most vital of issues.

Coming soon from Bradford Smith and Olivia Kimbrell Press™.

www.ingramcontent.com/pod-product-compliance
Lightning Source LLC
Chambersburg PA
CBHW051420090426
42737CB00014B/2763
9781939603579